PLANNING YOUR RETIREMENT

PLANNING YOUR RETIREMENT

DAVID HOBMAN

HAMLYN

First published in 1990 by
The Hamlyn Publishing Group Limited
a division of the Octopus Publishing Group
Michelin House, 81 Fulham Road,
London SW3 6RB

ISBN 0 600 56905 5

Printed in Great Britain by Collins, Glasgow

CONTENTS

Introduction

For many of us retirement may well last for longer than childhood or our working career. This makes it important to plan it well in order to make the most of it.

We may be lucky enough to have sufficient income so that we do not have to worry unduly about the future, and can pursue hobbies for which we have previously had little time, explore new activities at which we have always wanted to try our hand and, perhaps, give service in our community. Or, we may want to augment our pension with some paid work, even perhaps to start up a little business enterprise. If we know how to go about it, many of these things may be achieved: we explain how in this book.

We need to approach retirement sensibly, trying to avoid emotion about lost careers and the status which went with our job, whether we gave up when we wanted to, or were forced to go earlier than we had hoped or expected. Whilst it is true that if we were fortunate in our choice of career, work may have been absorbing and satisfying, for many people it was little more than a means to an end in earning a living. Much work can be boring and repetitive, even in the most interesting careers!

If we can manage to make both practical and psychological adjustments towards the leisure years, they can turn out to be the most interesting and fulfilling period of our life. 'Retirement' is, in any case, probably the wrong word to use for something which is just beginning. For the housewife, or perhaps now, the househusband, there is little change in daily routines apart from the novelty of having someone at home all day.

Of course, it won't all run smoothly. All life has its ups and downs; but many of the difficulties and, for some people, even the physical pain which can be associated with old age, can be reduced, if not prevented, by making plans at a stage when we are in a position to do something about the circumstances of our lives. It is true that there can be no real compensation for the human losses which are also eventually associated with the later stages of life; but even here, it is possible to make positive adjustments with a combination of personal strength and realism.

We also need to remember that, while some features of our retirement will have common characteristics with those of other people and there are useful lessons to be learnt from other people's successes and failures, we are all unique human beings, so the plans we make and the solutions to our problems which we seek, need to be our own. Thank goodness, we are so different. A world full of clones would be as dull as ditchwater!

All this means that much of the talk and some of the literature about ageing, which reflect other people's attitudes towards it and which lump us together, as though we were a single homogeneous group, can be very damaging. It can distort reality by creating stereotypes and assigning us roles which often set us aside as a race apart. We are portrayed sitting passively outside a rose-covered cottage waiting for something to happen. We are not the doers any more, but the done-by. Do not let them do it to us! Remember it is the life which lies ahead that matters. The past is over, whether it was good or bad. It cannot be relived. It is the future which counts. Use it well!

ONE

Managing Our Money

> *'Annual income twenty pounds, annual expenditure nineteen nineteen six, result happiness. Annual income twenty pounds, annual expenditure twenty pounds ought and six, result misery.'* Mr Micawber,
> DAVID COPPERFIELD.

Nowadays, the great majority of people approaching retirement will be able to look forward to a reasonably decent occupational pension, together with whatever state benefits are available, and possibly some private savings. Fifty per cent of the older population own their own home, so in one way and another, we may well have the assets on which to base a full life, without too many anxieties about where the next penny is coming from. However, that is not to say that any of us can afford not to be careful. We all need to make sure that we make the most of what we have, and that we can balance our books, as Mr Micawber put it so graphically.

There are three basic conditions which have to be met in planning our financial future. Firstly, we need to work out how to use what we have available to its best effect. Secondly, we need to keep close watch on our out-goings and to provide ourselves with the realistic budget for a system of planned expenditure. Thirdly, we have to hope that inflation is kept under control. We can do something about the first two conditions, but not much about the third, except as voters.

Of course, it is not possible to predict the long-term future with absolute certainty, but at least we can anticipate the way things are likely to go, and then review the situation regularly as time passes. In this way, we can make adjustments as circumstances change and whilst there are still various options open to us. Fulfilment in later life is, to some extent, influenced by the degree to which we remain in control of events, rather than allowing them to dictate what we can or cannot do.

Ten years is by no means too far ahead to start planning for retirement, and even just a year before the change comes is not too late to make some important decisions which might lead to a long-lasting improvement in our financial circumstances. If we are married, or have a partner, it is essential in financial planning, as in any other aspect of preparation for the future, to do it *jointly*.

After all, like it or not, one of us is going to outlive the other, and so we both have a right to know what to expect and to reach joint decisions. Historically, women have outlived men by about five years or more.

But whoever is the survivor should be able to expect the best possible future. This needs to be talked about and planned together. It does not have to be morbid, if there is genuine affection and respect.

Leaving things unsaid does not lead to a happy future for ourselves, and for those who follow. For example, if we are house owners do we want to make the most of the capital which may be available to us, in order to have comfort and financial security in our old age? Or do we prefer to deny ourselves the benefits which a large capital asset can offer, by setting it all aside for a younger relative, who may not actually want us to make this sacrifice in any case, and who will probably be in late middle age by the time any large legacy becomes available? As in any other situation, there are no right and wrong answers to questions of this nature. The im-

9

portant thing, however, is that they should be asked, and that conclusions should be reached by those most centrally involved.

Where Our Money Will Go

Any realistic estimate of the future has to take into account the income we can expect, from all sources, and how much we will need to spend on which items. Firstly, we must consider the essentials, such as light and heat. Then there are those things which help to make life more interesting and pleasurable, for example, holidays, entertainment, or presents for members of the family. It is worth listing them all at the beginning of our preparation for retirement – both the large obvious items, as well as the small ones.

What follows is a checklist of likely spending in retirement; use it as a starting point from which to make up your own, in relation to your own priorities. Do not forget to keep it up to date.

■ The community charge, or poll tax, which replaces the rates and which, unlike the rates, we must all pay (but see page 41).

■ Water rates, which include sewerage, and which are set to rise quite substantially.

■ Rent, if it applies.

■ Fuel costs, including electricity, gas, and coal. Here it is important to remember that consumption will probably increase in retirement as we begin to spend more time at home.

■ Telephone: here again, costs may go up. There will be no office 'phone any more and, with the advent of high technology, the telephone will become increasingly accessible to those with hearing loss for whom it is a very important medium of communication.

■ Postage: apart from business correspondence, as families separate through career changes and travelling becomes more difficult it is increasingly important to keep in touch by post.

■ Insurance of the home and its contents. It is possible that premiums may go down slightly. Once retired, we may be regarded as a lower risk, because we are likely to be at home for more of the time, and the house will be empty less often. However, there are still very substantial differences in the premiums for homes in those places which are regarded as relatively free of crime, and many of the inner-city areas.

■ Household repairs and decorations. This is where DIY enthusiasts come into their own; but some people are not cut out to undertake repairs and, in any case, there are jobs which will need professional skills and others which become more difficult with the passing years, especially those involving bending and stretching. Here, it is worth having a plan with a three- or five-yearly cycle, so that things do not get out of hand.

■ Food and drink bills are also likely to go up, because we will be eating more at home, although it is still important to go out from time to time! But to off-set the added expense of more food consumed in the home, there may now be more time to economize by using fewer convenience foods and to devote more time to real cooking for *both* partners.
□ Alcohol is fine in moderation, although the loss of stresses associated with work may lead to a reduction in the amount you drink.

■ Smoke if you must! But remember it is never too late to give up: even after years of smoking, your health can still be improved, and the chances of breathing comfortably in later life increased, quite apart from the blessing to relations and friends who will no longer have to endure a polluted environment. Here is an element in the budget which can really be reduced for the benefit of everyone.

■ Television, record player, tape deck, compact disc and video. These all need money to increase their range of use and for their replacement. It is not much use having a video or a music centre, if you have nothing to play on them!

■ Newspapers and magazines. It is important not to lose touch with the world, and to keep up with long-standing interests. But economies can be effected by sharing regular publications with other people, and getting theirs in exchange.

■ Transport. First of all, for people who own a *car*, there is the question about keeping it: for how long? And is it the right size for changing needs? For those who enjoyed the benefit of having a company car available when at work, there will be the additional expense of having to run one's own, without help for the first time: the expenses may come as a shock.

The true cost of running a car often leads to more self-deception than almost any other feature of our domestic life. Here, it is well worth looking at some of the publications produced by motoring associations to make sure all the items involved have been realistically covered. They range from the obvious such as tax and insurance to petrol and oil; but repairs and maintenance, as well as depreciation, are much more difficult to assess with any degree of accuracy, unless you really understand what goes on under the bonnet. In this connection, car maintenance courses for *both* partners may lead to very considerable economies in the long run.

□ Bus and rail travel should also be calculated, with the benefits of concessions which we can usually begin to enjoy from sixty onwards.

■ Recreation is one of the features of life in retirement

which should grow. After all, that is really what it is all about. The reward for a long working life should be opportunities to enjoy ourselves and do the things we have always wanted to do, but which escaped us through family responsibilities, working long hours or overtime, and keeping on top of things generally.

Leisure pursuits need not be very expensive; but they are an important feature of our lives, and they should be included in our budget under hobbies, classes, sports, gardening and social activities.

■ Holidays. A change of scenery in retirement is every bit as important as it was when we were younger. Older people are regarded as amongst the most interesting and adventurous explorers of new places and new experiences by one of the major travel companies.

■ Clothes are still important. We do not want to go on wearing the worn-out garments of years ago, just because we may no longer be so much involved in circles associated with people still at work. Women want to go on looking fashionable and so should men. So continue to budget for replacing clothes. In any case, some of us change our shape a bit from middle age onwards, so trying new sizes becomes more than just a luxury!

■ Keeping healthy also continues to cost money and, although the NHS is free for major items, there are still some treatments which have to be paid for. And, of course, if you are below the official pension age when you retire, you will still have to meet part of the cost for yourself. Some people will want to keep a medical insurance policy going. Changes in tax allowances are likely to make private health care insurance more attractive in retirement.

■ Presents. We all like to be givers as well as receivers, so the continued ability to give presents to friends and relatives does not change in retirement; but a budget on the amounts to be spent is a sensible precaution. Presents do not have to be bought at the most expensive stores. Searching for bargains can be fun, and presents which are made by the giver can also be the source of great pleasure. In some cases they can help hobbies to pay for themselves.

■ Pets. The companionship of animals can be very important in later life. They give us an excuse to talk to ourselves, and they don't argue! Dogs may continue to provide an important incentive to keep on walking; but they need feeding and they have their illnesses too, so it is just as well to budget for vet's bills, as well as the animal's keep.

■ Subscriptions. Many of us have long-standing memberships of professional, trade, or social groups which are important to keep us in touch; most offer reduced rates for members in retirement.

■ Charitable gifts. Some people like to keep up with charitable giving. Donations may have to be smaller on a reduced income in retirement than they were previously, but they continue to matter. If they are given through a four-year deed of covenant, the organizations on the receiving end can derive extra benefit by claiming back the income tax you paid on each £1 you give.

■ Life policies. These may need to be kept up, if benefits are not to be lost. Increasing numbers of people are now also taking out specially written policies designed to cover funeral expenses. These save the burden falling upon family members.

■ Regular savings. For some people, putting just something aside, however small the amount, continues to be important in providing a sense of security, and of having a nest egg to dip into against a rainy day. Crises can happen, in even the best regulated households, so it is sensible to have a budget item which can be used to cover the unexpected emergency.

Having worked out what we can expect, or hope to be able to spend, we then need to match it to the income we can anticipate. Then we can start cutting our coats according to our cloth. In undertaking the second part of the exercise, we need to take into account the various sources of income available to us. These are chiefly (1) *an occupational pension* (2) *state pension and other benefits* and (3) *other sources of income and capital which we may have at our disposal.*

Pensions

A pension of some kind or other, and quite probably from more than one source, is going to be the most important element in the incomes of most of us in our retirement. We have paid enough into the pension system during our working lives to provide this, so it is important to understand what is due to us and to make sure we get it.

There will also be the basic state pension and, in some cases, supplementary benefits from the state.

Occupational Pensions

For many of us, this will be the most important element in our retirement income. The majority of us moving into retirement, from now onwards, will have a pension from work, and, as going from one job to another becomes more common, some of us will take our entitlements with us. Others may have several sources of occupational pension; but the underlying principles in deciding how to make the most of this source of income remain the same.

Firstly, it is important to establish if the pension is based upon a proportion of *final earnings,* in which case it is fairly simple to work out what the amount is going to be. If it is what is known as a *money purchase scheme,* the money paid into the fund on our behalf by our employer together with our own contributions, will be added up to arrive at a global sum which can then be used to purchase an annuity.

Whatever form our pension arrangements at work may

take, we have a legal right to regular up-dated information about the scheme we are in. We must be given basic information about it, and we have a right to ask for, and to be given, copies of its legal and financial documentation (which we may be asked to pay for). We also have the right to ask for, and to be given, statements of the pension amounts and entitlement we have built up, as well as of the rights and choices we have in deciding how to use them to our best advantage. This information should be given to us by the scheme's manager.

If it is a *money purchase scheme,* we may expect to get a letter which might read something like this, although obviously, the amounts will differ from person to person:

The options open to you are as follows:

A) Personal Pension £13,721
    Widow's Pension £6,860

Or Alternatively

B) Cash Sum £30,179
    Balance Pension £10,762
    Widow's Pension £6,860

Using the approximate purchase price of A) above (£155,255) equal member and widow's pensions could be provided as follows:

Member's Pension and Widow's Pension £12,272

If you take the cash sum (as mentioned above) the approximate balance purchase price of £125,754 would provide equalized pensions as follows:

Member's Pension and Widow's Pension £9,938.

In the event, Mr X and his wife chose to take the capital sum of £30,179 to pay off a mortgage and provide a nest egg which they invested at the best rate they could find, at first in a building society and later in a bank. They accepted the reduced-rate pension of £9,938 because it would remain the same whichever partner survived the other. In their case, the pension had a built-in annual increase of 3 per cent to go some way towards inflation, if it reached that amount, and in most years the Pension Trustees were able to make up any difference with a voluntary contribution.

The questions to ask in calculating our future are:

■ as the pension is taxed at source, how much will it actually amount to in hard cash?

■ how much of the entitlement can be taken in advance as a tax-free capital sum, bearing in mind the fact that it will lead to a reduction in the amount of the pension we will then be paid? In any case, the maximum which can be taken in tax-free capital is 25 per cent of the whole amount, with a maximum of £150,000.

■ is it a joint scheme, in which our surviving partner may be entitled to the same level of income, for a reduced joint pension (as in the illustration on page 16)?

Of course, the differing ages of the partners will have a bearing on the amounts payable. For example, if the surviving wife (or husband, if the wife is the breadwinner) is twenty years younger than her partner in the scheme she (or he) will receive a good deal less than someone of about the same age. This is because the calculations, on which the amounts distributed are based, will naturally assume that payments to a much younger partner will continue for many years.

Specialized accountants, known as actuaries, spend their time in making calculations about how long we are likely to live. It might seem to be a slightly gloomy occupation, but it is very important that they should get their sums right!

■ another question to ask about the position of the survivor is what arrangements are made if the person who has earned the pension does not live long enough to enjoy it at all, or does not survive long in retirement? Here again, the deciding issue should take into account the arrangements made for the survivor.

■ is the pension index-linked and, if so, for how much? Some people, for example those working in the public sector, have been very fortunate in enjoying pensions which have kept up with inflation; but if, as in many schemes, there is no allowance, it will quickly slide in value as years pass when inflation may be running at 6 per cent or more.

In some cases, employers may make a voluntary additional contribution to bridge the difference; but it is very important to find out the precise position. And, while it is obviously helpful for a reasonable employer and the pension trustees to make up the difference, there can be no guarantee about what is going to happen in the future. Suppose the business ceases? The basic pension itself will be protected, but additional bonuses may come to an end.

Finding out about the extent of inflation proofing (if any) is, therefore, very important in calculating our likely future position in the long term. It could well influence decisions about whether to take a lump sum and invest it in a personal annuity. This might produce a better return than the actual pension scheme, for at least part of the capital.

One of the difficulties facing many of those who are now well into their retirement is the fact that they were not in a position to plan for inflation. Their occupational pensions, if they had any, were partly based upon pre-war earnings. These were very small in comparison with present-day money values, and there was no protection. Fortunately, for most of us the situation is now changing, but for people in the least attractive schemes, it may be important to make voluntary additional contributions for as long as possible in the last years at work (and you are allowed to put in up to 15 per cent), or to take out additional policies to augment the occupational scheme income. This is yet another reason why thinking about retirement well in advance and making plans for it are so important.

■ in making a budget for retirement income, it is useful to find out, in advance, how long we will have to wait for the first payment, as well as when and how payments are to be made on a regular basis.

■ it may also be worthwhile finding out whether we are likely to qualify for an occupational pension if we decide to retire early or if circumstances force us to give up our employment before we had anticipated.

Information about occupational schemes

There are several useful sources of information about occupational pension schemes. They include:

The Occupational Pensions Advisory Service, 8a Bloomsbury Square, London WC1A 2LP. This is an independent organization and is registered as a charity. It was set up to provide advice and assistance for individual enquirers.

Occupational Pensions Board, Lynwood Road, Thames Ditton, Surrey KT7 ODP. This is the government-established body which was set up chiefly to supervise occupational pension schemes, especially those which are contracted out of the State Earnings Related Pension Scheme (SERPS, see page 25). It publishes information leaflets, and can investigate a scheme if it is believed to be breaking parts of the regulating law, but it cannot take up individual enquiries.

The Company Pensions Information Centre, 7 Old Park Lane, London W1Y 3LJ. This is an independent centre supported by a number of insurance companies. It publishes free leaflets for members of pension schemes (but please send a large stamped envelope with any requests). It can provide general information, but will not become involved, or intervene, in disputes between individuals and particular pension schemes.

Other sources of information include local Citizens Advice Bureaux and Age Concern (see page 128).

Personal Pensions

Personal pension schemes are really savings plans, or policies, run by an insurance company, a bank, a building society or a unit trust scheme. They have to be officially approved, if they are running schemes which are 'contracted out' of the state scheme (SERPS, see page 25).

People who join these schemes pay regular premiums, or lump sums at greater intervals, and the money is then invested to provide a personal pension until the subscriber's death in much the same way as a money purchase scheme. Part of the accumulated money can usually be paid out as a tax-free lump sum on retirement, but once money has been invested in a scheme, it is usually impossible to withdraw it until retirement.

Nearly all personal pension policies offer an option to guarantee payment. If the pensioner dies within that period payments will be continued to a nominated dependent. Some insurance companies offer a widow's or widower's reversionary annuity. This can either be set at the same rate as the pensioner receives, or at a lower percentage.

Up to the age of 50, the maximum percentage of one's income that can be contributed to a personal pension scheme is 17.5 per cent. Above 50 the percentage allowed increases:

> 51 – 55, 20 per cent
> 56 – 60, 22.5 per cent
> 60 plus, 27.5 per cent.

Pension schemes run by employers are now voluntary and nobody can be forced to join them. If we decide to leave our employer's schemes, it is important to calculate the alternative benefits carefully. The older we are, the less likely it is that we will be able to get better terms by leaving the company scheme, without making a very large investment. We will also have to sacrifice the contributions made by our employer into our pension fund. So the best advice may be to stay put.

Self-employed people
Personal pensions are also used by self-employed people. You do not pay into SERPS. This means that if you do not pay for a personal pension you will only receive the basic state pension when you retire. Obviously, the earlier a personal pension is started the greater the benefits are going to be; but it is still better to start late in life rather than do nothing at all.

Information about personal pensions
There are several useful sources of information about personal pensions schemes. They include:

Association of British Insurers, Aldermary House, Queen Street, London EC4 1TT. This is the trade association of insurance companies. It publishes a series of general leaflets about pensions and life insurance.

British Insurance and Investment Brokers Association, BIIBA House, 14 Bevis Marks, London EC3 7NT. This can give you the names and addresses of member firms working locally. It also publishes a directory of insurance brokers for the UK.

The Campaign for Independent Financial Advice, 33 St John Street, London EC1M 4AA. This has an answering service on 01-200 3000 through which it can give you the names and addresses of independent intermediaries in your own area.

The State Pensions
Retirement pensions, which are taxable, are paid to people who have reached the official pension age. This is 60 for a woman and 65 for a man. They are paid at the same rate to everyone who has fulfilled the contribution conditions, and who is considered to be retired, as described below.

To qualify for the full rate of pension you must have paid, or been credited with, National Insurance contributions at the full rate, for most of the years of your working life. If you have not paid enough, you will probably receive a reduced pension, or possibly nothing at all. The term 'working life' means the number of tax years in which you are expected to pay, or have been credited with, contributions. The period normally starts when you are 16 and ends with the tax year in which you are 59, if you are a woman, or 64 for a man.

Married women, widows or divorcees may be able to use their husband's, or ex-husband's, contributions to qualify for a pension (see Widows' and widowers' benefits, page 28 and Divorce and separation, page 27).

If you qualify, your pension may then consist of a basic pension, plus an additional pension if you worked after April 1978, and a graduated pension if you worked between April 1961 and April 1975. In addition, you may receive an increased pension if you defer your retirement until you are older, or if you defer taking your pension for up to 5 years.

But you do not have to give up work entirely to be treated as retired for pension purposes. You may still qualify, if one or more of the following conditions apply:

- you are not doing any paid work.

- you expect to work only occasionally, or for not more than 12 hours a week, or under similar conditions.

Once a man has reached 70 and a woman 65, these rules do not apply any more.

If you are a married woman, you are entitled to a retirement pension based on your husband's contributions, when he retires and draws his pension, as long as you are over 60 yourself, and have retired from regular work, apart from 'domestic duties', or you have reached the age of 65.

If you are a woman and you qualify for a basic pension on your own and on your husband's contributions, you receive the pension on your own contribution. If it falls below a stated figure, because you only paid full contributions for part of your working life, or only paid the married woman's reduced contribution, you will have to wait until your husband retires. When your husband draws his pension, you can then claim the married woman's pension at the full rate, as long as your husband has a complete contribution record. Otherwise, it will be less.

If you are the husband of a woman who is under 60 when you retire at 65 or over, you may claim for your wife as a dependent. Your pension will then be increased. If your wife is earning, or is in receipt of an occupational pension in her own right, you will not be able to claim an increase for her on your pension.

If you are a wife, receiving a retirement pension, you may be able to get an increase for your husband if he is not getting a pension of his own. However, you can only claim this increase if you were already receiving an addition for your husband with unemployment, sickness, or invalidity benefit immediately before retiring.

Special conditions apply for married women who worked during the war. If you are one, and you paid enough contributions into the state scheme, which can be credited towards a pension, and you were working during the week beginning 7 January 1946, you may be eligible. If this is the case, it is worth contacting your local Social Security office to explain when and where you worked. They will need to know your National Insurance number so that they can trace your records.

If the pension comes to more than £1 per week, and you live in this country, you can choose to have it paid:

- weekly, by a book of orders which can be cashed at the post office of your choice. In this case, you must cash the order within three months of the date shown on it.

- every four weeks, or every thirteen weeks in arrears, direct into a bank or building society account.

Pensions of £1 weekly, or less, are paid annually in arrears.

Protecting your pension

You cannot receive the state pension until you reach the official pension age of 60 for a woman and 65 for a man; but it is important to make sure you have paid sufficient contributions to receive the full pension when you do reach the appropriate age.

If you are drawing a benefit, such as unemployment or invalidity, credits will be put on your entitlement record. If you are under 60 and available for work, it may be worthwhile signing on as unemployed, even if you are not entitled to benefit. This is in order to get the credits on your record. If you are a man between 60 and 64, you will automatically receive credits, even though you are not signing on for benefits.

If you are in any doubt about your contribution record, it is worth checking at your local Social Security office. If you then find you are not entitled to credits, and are going to end up with an incomplete National Insurance record, it may be worth your while to consider paying voluntary contributions.

Going abroad

If you go abroad for less than three months, you can cash all your pension orders when you get back to this country; but as a pension cannot be cashed more than three months after it is date-stamped, you must tell the Social Security office, well in advance, if you are going to be abroad for a longer period.

If you decide to go and live abroad permanently, or are going to be out of the UK for more than three months, you can receive the pension in the country where you are going to live; but you may not get any increase when the pension goes up. However, increases can be paid if you are going to live within the countries of the Common Market, or in certain others where the government has agreed arrangements. These are: Australia, Austria, Belgium, Bermuda, Canada, Cyprus, Denmark, Finland, France, Federal Republic of Germany, Gibraltar, Greece, Iceland, Irish Republic, Israel, Italy, Jamaica, Jersey and Guernsey, Luxembourg, Malta,

Mauritius, Netherlands, New Zealand, Norway, Portugal, Spain, Sweden, Switzerland, Turkey, USA and Yugoslavia.

SERPS

SERPS, the State Earnings-Related Pension Scheme, is an additional amount, within the pension, for those who contributed towards it from the time it was introduced in 1978. If you contributed, you may qualify for an additional pension, even if you are not entitled to the basic pension.

The majority of company pension schemes have 'contracted out' of SERPS. They are allowed to do this if they offer equal or better terms and have satisfied the Occupational Pensions Board, which then issues them with a certificate of approval.

If you are in a 'contracted-out' scheme, you will get no additional state pension; but most contracted-out schemes pay a guaranteed minimum pension which is broadly equivalent to the additional state pension you would otherwise have received.

The government has announced quite far-reaching changes in SERPS; but these will not come into full effect until the year 2000, and they will not affect anyone retiring before then.

If you are a widow, you can inherit your husband's additional pension and add it to your own. In the same way, if you are a widower, you can claim on your late wife's entitlement, if you were both over pensionable age at the time of the death. But there is a limitation on the amount which you will receive in these circumstances. It must not be more than the maximum additional pension which a single person would expect to receive.

Graduated pension

A number of people who are now retiring will probably also have some entitlement to the graduated pension. This stems from payments you made between 1961 and 1975. The graduated pension will not be affected by any earnings you may have after 65 for a man, and 60 for a woman. You can also draw any graduated pension to which you are entitled, even if you do not qualify for a basic pension.

If you are a wife, you can only draw a graduated pension in respect of your own graduated contributions but, if you are a widow over 60, and you are receiving a retirement pension, you can receive graduated pension. This is in addition to your basic retirement pension. It is equal to a half of the graduated pension your husband was receiving, or had earned, when he died. You can also receive the graduated pension to which you were entitled, in your own right, through contributions you made.

If you are widowed before you are 60, you can receive a graduated pension when you reach 60 and retire; whether it is based on your own, or your late husband's contributions. If you are a widower, you can inherit half the graduated pension earned by your wife's contributions, in addition to any for which you have contributed yourself, as long as you were both over pension age when she died.

Early retirement

If you retire early, before the official retirement date, you may qualify for unemployment, sickness and invalidity benefit; or possibly for income support and housing benefit. But, you will also want to make sure that you protect your rights to your state pension.

Unemployment benefit, which is taxable, depends on whether you have paid sufficient National Insurance contributions. It can be paid for a maximum of 52 weeks. The amount you will get will be reduced if you are over 55 and are receiving payment through an occupational pension.

To qualify, you have to be unemployed but be capable of and available for work. You may be disqualified from unemployment benefit for up to 26 weeks, if you leave a job voluntarily without what is officially known as 'just cause'.

You may also be disqualified if you choose to accept early retirement; but this does not apply if you are made redundant.

If you have to retire as a result of ill health, you may be entitled to sickness pay for the first 28 weeks, and then to invalidity benefit.

If your savings and income fall below a stated amount, you may be entitled to income support and/or community charge benefit.

Continuing to work

If you are a man aged below 70 or a woman below 65 and you are in receipt of a retirement pension, even if you go on working after pension age, you will no longer have to pay national insurance contributions.

Divorce and separation

Once your divorce is made absolute, it is very important to inform your local Social Security office as soon as possible. This is partly because once your marriage has ended, you will want to ensure you pay National Insurance contributions to protect your own right to benefit, and especially to the retirement pension.

If you cannot get a full pension based on your own contributions, you may be able to use your former husband's, or wife's, contribution to raise your basic pension entitlement to the maximum single person's pension. This will only apply if you reached pension age, or were divorced, after April 1979. But you are not entitled to your former husband's, or wife's, graduated or additional pension.

If you are under the pension age when you divorce, you can substitute your former husband's, or wife's, contribution record for your own from the start of your working life, or from the date your marriage started, until the time the marriage ended. Then, depending on your age, you may need to pay additional contributions after your divorce in order to qualify for a full pension.

If your divorce takes place after you reach pension age, you can use your husband's, or wife's, contribution record in the same way as described for a divorce which takes place under the pension age.

If you decide to re-marry before you reach the pension age, you cannot claim a pension on your first husband's, or wife's, contributions; but, if you remarry after you have reached the pension age, you will not lose your entitlement to any retirement pension you may get based on your previous husband's, or wife's, contributions.

If you are separated, and do not qualify for a pension on your own contributions, you may be able to claim the married woman's pension; but, you cannot do this until your husband claims his pension.

Widows' and widowers' benefits
There are three main benefits which you may claim if you are a widow, depending upon your circumstances. They are:

- widow's payment, a once-only, tax-free lump sum.

- widow's pension, which is taxable.

- widowed mother's allowance, which is taxable.

If you are widowed, you may be able to claim a widow's payment, and, at the same time, a widowed mother's allowance, or a widow's pension. However, you cannot get a widowed mother's allowance and a widow's pension at the same time. You will be eligible for the widow's payment if you are under 60, if your husband was under 65, or if he was over 65 but was not getting a state retirement pension when he died.

Your widow's benefits are based on your husband's National Insurance contributions. They are not based upon your contributions. You cannot get any widow's benefits on your former husband's National Insurance if you had been divorced before he died; if you were living with a man as though you were married to him, without being legally married; or if you are living with another man, as though you were married to him.

You can only get a widow's benefit if your husband had paid sufficient National Insurance contributions, and the rules about the number that are needed can be very complicated. You may want to consult your local National Insurance office.

You may get a widow's pension if your husband had paid enough National Insurance contributions and you must be over 45 when your husband died. You may also receive an additional pension based on your husband's earnings since April 1978; but if you receive a guaranteed minimum pension from your husband's occupational scheme, your widow's pension may be reduced by this amount.

When you reach pension age and retire, you may then be entitled to a retirement pension based on your husband's contributions, in place of your widow's pension. You may also get half of your husband's graduated pension.

Your widow's pension will not be affected by your earnings. But, if you decide to put off your retirement and go on working after the age of 60, you will not earn any extra pension, unless you give up the widow's pension.

If you re-marry, you will lose the widow's pension. It will also be stopped during any period when you live with a man as his wife.

You may be entitled to a widowed mother's allowance if your husband paid enough National Insurance contributions and you are receiving child benefit for one of your children, or your husband was receiving child benefit, or if you are expecting your husband's child.

This benefit is usually paid for as long as you would normally be receiving child benefit.

If you are a widower, and you get a retirement pension of less than the full rate, you may be able to get an increased amount by using your wife's National Insurance contributions as long as you were both over pension age when she died. You may also inherit half of your wife's graduated pension, and you can add her additional pension to yours up to the maximum additional amount allowed for a single person.

When you register your husband's, or wife's, death the Registrar of Deaths will give you a registration certificate and a form which you should send to the local Social Security office. They will then, in turn, send you the claim form which you must complete.

Christmas bonus
A bonus of £10, which has remained unchanged for many years, is paid to you if you are receiving the retirement pension, or one of a number of other benefits.

The bonus is paid in the first full week of December. It is tax free, and has no effect on any other benefit. You will receive it if you are living in this country, or in any EEC country and there is usually no need to claim for it. It will either be included in your order book, if you collect your pension from the post office, or paid directly into your account with your pension.

Other State Benefits

If fortune smiles on us, we may not have to lay claim to most of the complex range of social security benefits which now exist. They are designed to meet the needs of people suffering from particular disabilities of health or poverty, and apart from the retirement pension itself, there are very few we are likely to call upon, or need to understand.

However, things can go wrong, even in the best regulated families, and our circumstances can change overnight so it is just as well to have an idea of what is available, and the personal circumstances in which we are entitled to claim for what are, after all, the rights of citizenship. There is no shame in seeking financial help through a system to which we have contributed during the whole of our working life.

The state benefit system is extremely complicated and the

rates of many of the benefits change from year to year. What we have set out to do in this section is to explain the basis on which they are calculated, in the hope that we have alerted you to the fact that you may be entitled to help and to remind you that it is yours by right.

We have also suggested sources of help and advice, where you should be able to obtain more precise calculations of what you may get.

Income Support

Income support is the system which has taken the place of supplementary benefits and supplementary pensions. It is really designed for unemployed people; those who are over 60 and who do not have sufficient money to live on; those who are too ill to work; and those who are staying at home to look after a disabled relative. It is not taxable. Income support may still be available to you if you have a certain amount of savings (but in 1989, not more than £6,000), own your own home, and have not paid National Insurance contributions.

In normal circumstances, you cannot claim income support if you are working for more than 24 hours a week, or if you have a partner who is. For this purpose, 'partner' means the person to whom you are married, or the person with whom you are living as though you were married.

The amount of income support you are likely to receive depends mainly on how much the government decides people must have to live on, and how much other income you have from social security benefits or part-time work.

If you are not sure whether you are entitled to income support it may be worth your while to claim because, even if you are only entitled to a very small amount from this source, you will, by receiving it, automatically become eligible for other benefits such as free dental treatment, help with glasses, wigs and fabric supports, help with fares to hospital if you are going for treatment, lump-sum payments from the Social Fund, and grants for insulation.

Some forms of savings and capital are taken into account to calculate if you are below the qualifying level or not. These include cash; money in the bank or building society, including current accounts that pay no interest; national savings; premium bonds; stocks and shares; and half of any joint savings you have with someone else. However, the Department of Social Security will ignore the value of your home, if you own it; the surrender value of a life insurance policy; and arrears of attendance allowance, mobility allowance or income support for up to 52 weeks.

In working out your income, the Department of Social Security will include your earnings, state benefits, occupational pensions, and any other money you may be receiving after tax and National Insurance contributions have been made. For a couple, both your incomes will be added together. But some income will be ignored. This includes mobility allowance; attendance allowance; actual interest from savings or capital, below an upper ceiling, and final earnings when you retire. The Department of Social Security will ignore certain other elements of your income as well.

Payment from income support comes under two headings:

■ firstly, what is assessed by the government to be the amount that people in different circumstances need to live on to cover their normal needs.

■ secondly, there are premiums for groups of people who have special needs. If you qualify for more than one premium, you can normally expect to receive only the one which would give you the most money. However, if you receive any of the following premiums you may also be entitled to any other for which you apply successfully: family premium; disabled child's premium; or severe disability premium.

Special premiums are paid to people in respect of the following conditions:

■ if you are a parent with at least one child.

■ if you have a child who is getting either the attendance allowance or the mobility allowance, you may be entitled to the family premium.

■ if you have a child who is registered blind, you may be entitled to the disabled child's premium.

■ if you are bringing up one or more children on your own, you may be entitled to the lone parent premium.

■ if you, or your partner, are between 60 and 79, you may be entitled to the pensioner premium.

■ if you, or your partner, are over 60 and getting the attendance allowance, or the mobility allowance, or invalidity benefit, or the severe disablement allowance, or are registered blind, you may be entitled to the higher pensioner premium.

■ if you, or your partner, are 80 or over, you may be entitled to the higher pensioner premium, though at time of writing this is very small (25p).

■ if you, or your partner, are getting certain benefits because you are disabled or cannot work because you suffer from a long-term illness or disability and, for example, are in receipt of invalidity benefit, severe disablement allowance, mobility allowance, or attendance allowance, you may be entitled to the disability premium.

■ if you, or your partner, are registered blind, you may be entitled to the disability premium.

■ if you, or your partner, have been certified sick for at least 28 weeks, you may be entitled to the disability premium.

■ if you are living alone and getting attendance allowance, but no-one is getting the invalid care allowance for looking after you, the severe disability pension may be paid, as well as the disability premium or the higher pension premium.

You may also be entitled to help with housing costs if you are paying back a mortgage, home loan, or loan for essential repairs or certain improvements to your home. If you, or your partner, are over 60, you may get an amount added on to cover all the interest that you have to pay. If you, and your partner, are under 60 you may get an amount added on to cover half the interest you have to pay for the first sixteen weeks after you start getting income support. After this sixteen-week period is over, an amount to cover all the interest will normally be added on. An amount is also added on if you have to pay ground rent (feu duty in Scotland) or certain service charges.

Local councils are responsible for paying community charge benefit to help people on income support. This benefit is described on pages 41-3.

The Social Fund

There may be circumstances in your retirement which would qualify you for help from the Social Fund. The Social Fund was introduced by the government to replace the previous system of single supplementary benefit payments to help people meet exceptional expenses which would be difficult, if not impossible, to meet from regular income. It also replaces maternity and death grants.

The following payments can be made from the Social Fund:

■ interest-free loans, designed to assist you if you have been on income support for at least 26 weeks and you need essential items which you could not, otherwise, afford and which you cannot budget for from your normal income. They would normally be provided for an item which would be considered to be of a high priority. For example, it might be for the expenses of a move to more appropriate accommodation, for redecoration, clothing or furniture.

The loan has to be repaid, and any savings, above quite a low figure, are taken into account before the loan is made.

■ crisis loans, which are available to anyone, whether you are receiving income support or not. As the name implies, they are there for an unpredicted emergency – a fire or a flood, for example – and there is serious risk to your health or safety. They are also interest-free and repayable. In assessing the amount of loan to be made, account will be taken of your savings and income, as well as of any other possible sources of help.

■ community care grants, which do not have to be repaid. 'Elderly people with restricted mobility' are amongst those who are considered to be high priority for these grants. Savings above quite a low figure are taken into account, if a grant is to be made under one of the four following headings:

□ help with moving out of institutional or residential care, for example, for a bed, a cooker, fuel connection or for removal charges.

□ help to remain within the community, for example, minor house repairs, bedding or essential furniture.

□ help with exceptional pressures on families, which may be caused by disability, chronic sickness or a breakdown in a relationship.

□ help with urgent travel expenditure, for example, to visit someone who is in hospital or to attend a funeral.

■ payment for maternity needs, if you are on income supplement or family credit.

■ funeral payments, if you are responsible for the costs of a funeral and either you or your partner are in receipt of income support or community charge benefit; you can apply to the Social Fund for a payment towards the basic costs of a simple funeral. Savings, as well as any money from the estate of the person who has died, such as insurance policies, will be taken into account. The amount you may be awarded will depend upon your resources.

Claims must normally be lodged within three months of the funeral; but it is probably just as well to find out beforehand whether you are likely to be eligible.

■ cold weather payments may be made, in certain circumstances, to cover the costs of additional fuel during every week of cold weather, if you are receiving income support, are over 60, and have very low savings.

You will know if the payment is going to be made because the local Social Security office will declare it to be a period of cold weather, for purposes of the payment, when the average temperature is 0°Centigrade, or below, for seven consecutive days.

Loans and grants from the Social Fund are *discretionary,* and the funds available are limited so decisions about the award of a grant or loan are made by a Social Fund Officer. If you are dissatisfied with the Social Fund Officer's decision you can ask for a review.

Payments for funeral costs, and in respect of cold weather, are governed by *regulations* which state who is entitled to receive them and in what circumstances. They are, therefore, not affected by budget constraints, or decisions made at the discretion of Social Fund Officers.

Invalidity Benefit

This benefit, which is not taxable, is paid to you if you have been unable to work for at least 28 weeks. It depends upon whether you have paid National Insurance contributions; but it does not take your savings or other income into account. It comprises a number of different elements, of which the most important part is the basic invalidity pension. If you do not qualify for this, you will not be entitled to any other parts of the benefit.

If the circumstances of your invalidity are such that it is

accepted you will not work again, the benefit continues into your 'official' retirement.

The invalidity allowance, which is added on to the basic invalidity benefit, is provided to help people who became invalids more than five years before they would normally have retired. It is, itself, divided into three rates, depending upon your age at the time when you first became unable to work.

To qualify, you must already have been entitled to sickness benefit; but if you do not qualify, you may be eligible for a severe disablement allowance.

Mobility Allowance

This benefit, which is not taxable, is for people who cannot walk at all, or who have great difficulty in walking. It is intended to help you with movement outside your home. You can spend it in any way you want and you do not have to explain how you spend it.

The mobility allowance does not depend upon National Insurance contributions, or the amount of savings and income you have. If it is awarded to you it will not affect any other benefit or pension you may be getting.

To qualify, you have to have been unable to walk because of a physical disability for at least a year before the age of 65, whether you are a man or a woman; but your claim must be in the hands of the Department of Social Security and approved by them before your sixty-sixth birthday. If you continue to qualify for the allowance, it will be paid until you reach the age of 75.

If you are a car owner, and you get the mobility allowance, you will be exempt from road tax. If you do not own your own car, you may be able to get one through the special scheme run by Motability. This is a registered charity which offers leasing and hire purchase facilities. Its address is Motability, 2nd Floor, Gate House, Westgate, Harlow, Essex CM20 1HR.

Attendance Allowance

This benefit, which is not taxable, is for anyone from a child of two upwards, who is severely physically or mentally disabled and who needs regular attention or supervision. It does not depend upon your other benefits, or pensions you may be receiving; but it is taken into account if you apply for income support to help with fees in a residential care or nursing home.

To qualify, you must be so disabled that you either require regular attention throughout the day, with your normal bodily functions, or regular supervision is required to avoid putting the patient, or those involved in providing care, in any sort of danger. Or, you may need regular support during the night. In this case, the qualifying condition is based upon prolonged and repeated attention, and if someone else is required to remain awake regularly or for regular or extended periods. If you require help during the day and night, you may qualify for the allowance at a higher rate.

In the case of this benefit, medical conditions have to be satisfied for six months before the allowance will be paid; but you are entitled to apply after three months so that the allowance will begin after six months. If you are receiving the allowance and go into hospital or a council-run home, or if the council is paying for your support in a voluntary home, it will be stopped after four weeks.

If you are in receipt of a war or disablement pension, or a benefit which is paid under the terms of a special workman's compensation scheme, you may be entitled to a constant attendance allowance; but, in this case, the amount paid may be affected.

Invalid Care Allowance

This benefit, which is subject to tax, is normally paid to you if you are under the pension age, but are unable to work because you are looking after a severely disabled person.

The person for whom you are caring does not have to be a

relative and you do not have to be living in the same house. The conditions are that you must be over 16 and that you spend at least 35 hours a week in caring. It does not matter if you are married or single, but the person you are looking after does have to be in receipt of the attendance allowance, or the constant attendance allowance.

If you receive the invalid care allowance when you reach pension age, the amount will be adjusted to take into account any retirement pension you may be getting. If the rate of the pension is more than the rate of the invalid care allowance, this benefit will stop.

Appealing Against Social Security Decisions

The majority of decisions about social security are made by adjudication officers and, if you disagree with a decision, you are entitled to appeal to a Social Security Appeal Tribunal. This is independent of the Department of Social Security. If the decision involves a medical condition, it will be made by a medical practitioner or a medical board. In this case, you can go to a Medical Appeal Tribunal if you disagree with the decision.

If you want to make an appeal, you must write to the local Social Security office within three months of receiving a decision; in exceptional circumstances, a later appeal may be accepted if there is good reason for making it.

Your letter should say which decision you are appealing against and, as the letter will be included with the appeal papers, it is probably useful to set out the basis of your case at the outset. In some cases, the adjudication officer may actually change his original decision on the basis of this letter if you are able to provide significant facts which had not been taken into account before.

If you are not too sure about how to present your case, a local welfare rights agency, or the Citizens Advice Bureau will probably be able to help you prepare it, and to represent you at the tribunal.

When your letter has been received, you will be told when and where the tribunal will take place. Your case will be assessed by three independent people who are not connected with the Department of Social Security, and there will also be an adjudication officer present, but not the one who dealt with your original application and made the decision against which you are appealing.

You will be given time to put your case at the tribunal, which is quite informal, and you will also be asked questions by the members. At the end, you will be reimbursed for your travel expenses and you will either be told the result of your appeal straightaway, or it will be sent to you later if it is at all complicated. The job of the tribunal is to decide whether the original decision was correct in law, not whether it seemed fair or not.

You can also ask for a review, at any time, if you think the Social Security office did not have all the facts at its disposal, or it may have misunderstood some of the facts, and your circumstances may have changed since you made your original application. If you want the Social Security office to review your case, simply write giving your reasons. If the decision is against a review, you can still appeal against this decision.

Information About Social Security
There are several useful sources of information, and publications explaining the regulations in greater detail, which give up-to-date facts about the actual amounts of money involved. They include:
Age Concern England, Bernard Sunley House, 60 Pitcairn Road, Mitcham, Surrey CR4 3LL;
Age Concern Scotland, 33 Castle Street, Edinburgh, EH2 3DN;
Age Concern Wales, 4th floor, 1 Cathedral Street, Cardiff, South Glamorgan CF1 3BJ;
Age Concern Northern Ireland, 6 Lower Crescent, Belfast BT7 1NR.

Age Concern publishes annually *Your Rights (£1.50)*, a guide to money benefits for retired people. It can be ordered from the Marketing Department, Age Concern England, or obtained from many book shops. (See page 128 for telephone numbers.)

The Department of Social Security provides a Freephone advice and information service on all social security benefits on 0800 666 555. For overseas enquiries, apply to the Department of Social Security, Overseas Branch PMT52, Newcastle Upon Tyne NE98 1YX.

Local enquiries can be made at your nearest Citizens Advice Bureau or Age Concern group.

Publications and leaflets about each of the different benefits and the conditions which apply to them can be obtained from the local office of the Department of Social Security.

The National Federation of Retirement Pensions Association (Pensioners Voice), 14 St Peter Street, Blackburn, Lancs. BB2 2HD, publishes *Your Pension* (£1.25) each year.

Community Charge Benefit

This is the help for which you can claim in respect of rent and the community charge. It is not taxable and is operated by local councils.

When the community charge (or poll tax) replaced the rating system, rebates on the charge continued to be based upon the same system as applied for housing benefit. The change was automatic, so people did not need to reapply.

Basically, you can expect to get community charge benefit (that is a rebate on your community charge), if you have a low income, and have to pay either rent or the community charge. It makes no difference whether you are at work or not, and you do not need to have paid any National Insurance contributions. You may be single, or you may have a partner. You may live alone, or with your family, and it does not matter whether you live in council housing, private rented accommodation, your own home, a hotel, a guest house or other similar

41

type of accommodation.

Community charge benefit is there to meet the element of the rent which you have to pay simply to live in your home. It is known as the 'eligible rent' and it may not be the same amount that you pay your landlord.

Eligible rent may include some, or all, of the following: furniture, fuel for communal areas, cleaning of communal areas, portering, entry phone, caretakers and wardens, and emergency alarm systems. It cannot help with mortgage interest repayments, the cost of meals included in the rent, water charges, personal laundry and cleaning, ground rent and service for your home, if the lease was originally for more then 21 years, and rates for business premises.

You may qualify if you have a low income, not more than £8,000 in savings, and are responsible for paying rent. If you are a house-owner, you may get community charge benefit, but you will not get help with mortgage payments or service charges, which may be covered by income support.

If you are a tenant of a local council, a housing association, or a private landlord, you may be eligible for help with the community charge, rent and service charges.

If your landlord is a close relative and you share the household, you will not qualify; but if you live separately and only share areas like the hall or bathroom, you will be entitled to claim. Even if your landlord is a close relative, you make your claim in the normal way.

If you are a boarder, you may claim for community charge benefit in respect of the accommodation element in the charges you meet, and you may also get income support.

If you are in private residential care or a nursing home, you may get help with the rental element in the charges you meet; unless you are receiving income support. But, if you are in a home run by your local council, you cannot get community charge benefit.

If you are a joint home-owner or tenant, you may be eligible for community charge benefit towards the costs for which you are responsible.

Community charge benefit is paid for in one of two main ways. If you pay rent to your local council, your community charge benefit entitlement is taken off the full amount you would otherwise owe. If you pay rent to a private landlord, your community charge benefit is paid direct to the landlord.

The rules and qualifications for community charge benefit are quite complicated. If you think you might be eligible, you would be well advised to seek guidance from your local council, Citizens Advice Bureau, or Housing Advice Centre.

Savings and Investments

However far away retirement may seem, a realistic financial plan which makes the most of what we have – or can expect to have – will have a considerable impact on the quality of life during what may well be a long period of our lives.

Before starting to make any sort of long-term plan about how to make the best use of our capital assets, it is important to understand the fundamental difference between savings and investments.

Money *saved* with, say, a bank or building society earns interest. This fluctuates according to market rates, and is taxed at source. It is really a return for the money we are lending to the financial institution. We may decide to spend the interest as it is paid, in which case our capital will remain the same size; although if we do not have need to call on it immediately, we might decide to leave the interest so the amount we have deposited will grow. But the original sum saved does not, itself, get any larger.

In this connection, if we are going to continue to save the interest, it is worth looking for an account which calculates and pays it out four times a year. In this way, the interest itself gathers interest and the account will be more profitable than one which only pays out annually.

On the other hand, if we *invest* money we are, in essence, backing an enterprise which we believe will prosper or, in the case of unit trusts, putting it into a scheme run by managers who will then invest our money in a number of companies. Investing is, therefore, risky. Our shares may go up or down. However, if the companies in which we invest are successful, we are likely to benefit in two ways: firstly, through the dividends which will be declared once or twice a year; secondly, because the actual value of the shares will also increase.

For some people, investing is an exciting business. But even with knowledge of the system and insights into which products, or services, are likely to become increasingly popular the risks remain. It would certainly be a mistake to use too much capital in this way.

The most sensible course of action is probably to divide the money we have to save or invest, amongst a range of different types of institutions and accounts. We also want to make sure that some of our funds can be called in immediately, when we need them, although others can be less accessible, as part of a long term plan. In the long run, those which take more time to withdraw are likely to produce higher returns.

The regularity of interest payments, or dividends, may also be a factor in our choice, depending upon how urgently we need regular income payments to augment our pension. Some only pay twice, or even once a year.

Here again, *planning* is the keyword. Even though our income may be reduced in retirement, our outgoings may also go down. Our mortgage may be paid off, and with children grown-up and off the wing, we may find for the first time in thirty years we actually do have a little money to spare!

But then we have to ask whether the money being put aside is to pay for a holiday or repairs to our house within a year or so. Or is it towards a more distant time ahead, when we think the relative value of our pension may have declined, and our expenses on, say, health care or private transport may have to increase? The answers to these questions will have a bearing on whether we look for short-term gains or long-term growth in the money we put aside to work for us.

Having an emergency fund on which to call is certainly a good idea. But opinions about what size it ought to be vary greatly from perhaps £500 to the equivalent of three months' of our outgoings. The right figure may well lie somewhere between the two. Probably the best place to put this emergency fund is either in a high-interest bank or building society account. The market is now very competitive, and it makes good sense to shop around for the best place to lodge these funds.

We should also remember that we are free agents. We can shift our money around as we please. The days of having to face the rather awe-inspiring presence of the bank manager are definitely over! He is now working hard, in competition with everyone else, to woo us. He actually wants us to borrow money, not to lecture us on the virtues of thrift. In some instances, banks now even charge a fee for a consultation with the local branch manager!

Before we begin to plan where and how we will spread our funds, it is sensible to try and answer a number of questions:

- are we saving for the short or long term?

- are we likely to want some of our money out at quite short notice?

- how regularly do we want interest or dividend payments made?

- do we want to leave the money to grow, or do we need it to augment our regular income?

- what are the minimum and maximum amounts allowed for investing or saving in different schemes?

- what effect will our savings or investments have on our tax situation?

- are the dividends or interest paid with tax deducted?

- what sort of protection exists for our money?

And then, perhaps the most difficult question of all to answer:

- what risk, if any, are we prepared to take, in the hope of making a greater profit in the end?

Savings

Life insurance savings schemes will be among the first we are likely to consider, in relation to any long-term plan. Most of them have a minimum term of about ten years. They will either comprise a with-profit endowment policy or be linked to a unit trust. Endowments become more valuable as time passes, although the insurance companies will never guarantee the amounts of growth. On the other hand, unit trusts may go up or down.

Whilst life insurance is, presumably, taken out with a particular beneficiary in mind, with a with-profits endowment policy, if we are still alive at the end of the term, we can recover the sum assured for ourselves, together with all the profit bonuses which have been declared and have accrued.

Unit trust saving schemes sometimes produce considerable growth, especially over a long period of time, but there is a risk attached to them because their value can go down, as well as up.

National Savings provide an absolutely safe place to put money aside, though their return is normally quite modest, unless we pay tax at a high rate. The recently introduced capital bonds, which pay high interest without any deduction of tax at source, are a good form of savings if we have no tax liability.

National Savings offer a variety of ways to place our money from ordinary and investment accounts, which offer better returns, but take longer to get our money out; to savings certificates; income bonds; deposit bonds and, of course, 'Ernies' premium bonds, which might be regarded as a respectable form of gambling.

British government stocks, through which the country borrows money from us, its citizens, are known as 'gilts', or 'gilt-edged', and give a guaranteed return. They produce interest on the way, and can be reclaimed at the same value as that at which they were originally issued, at the end of an agreed period attached to them at the time of their issue. This may be five, ten, fifteen or more years. But as their value fluctuates, within the period of their time span, in relation to inflation, interest rates and the general state of the economy, they can be bought and sold at a profit or a loss, depending upon which way the market is going. They can be purchased through post offices.

Corporation stocks work in the same way as government stocks; but they are not guaranteed by the government and they are not for sale at post offices. They are created to assist local councils, or other public utilities, to raise additional funds which they may need beyond the income they can derive from the community charge, or their normal sources of revenue. They are traded through the Stock Exchange.

Some cities and counties raise money directly through their own bonds. These are advertised in the press with their current rates of interest. They are not traded on the Stock Exchange. Normally, it is not possible to cash in a bond before the end of its contracted period. If it is allowed, there will probably be a penalty.

Building societies are changing rapidly. One, at least, has become more like a bank, and others may well follow. They now offer a wide range of savings accounts. Some sell unit trusts and they may even deal in stocks and shares.

Investments

Stocks and shares are, of course, the most risky investments to put our money into but, by the same token, they are also potentially the most valuable, if they are successful. They will probably provide income twice a year and their value can increase very substantially overnight; but they can fluctuate from day to day, and they are certainly not investments for the nervous or faint-hearted to be trying.

They are also a gamble, so we may not want to invest as a matter of principle. If we do, we may want to be very careful about which companies in which to invest, in relation to the products they make, or the places in which they trade. They may relate to the manufacture of armaments, or tobacco products; or in trading with regimes of which we may disapprove. Moral scruples will differ for all of us.

At any rate, if we do decide to invest in the stock market, it certainly makes sense to spread the risk by putting our money into a number of different companies.

Unit trusts are obviously less risky than purchasing shares direct. This is because the unit trust managers spread their investments over a broad range of companies, perhaps choosing ones that are trading in the same part of the world or in the same country, or perhaps going for companies making similar products. Other groupings may be in relation to size, or potential for growth.

Unit trusts can usually be bought in a lump sum, or by regular monthly investments. When an outright payment is involved, there will be a minimum amount: this is usually £500; although some may require less.

Unit trusts will also offer different funds which are either designed to produce as much income as possible in the short term, or to grow in value over a number of years; but however skilled their advisers and managers may be, they have no magic wands and, in the final analysis, our guess, or a hunch about the way things may go, will sometimes turn out to be just as good as the experts'. They are certainly careful to make no promises about the ways in which the funds they offer are likely to perform and their claims are always based on past performance.

Unit trusts have to be registered, and they now have an independent ombudsman for complaints.

Investment trusts may provide a useful compromise between the direct purchase of shares and investment in a unit trust.

The investment trust is, itself, a company quoted on the Stock Exchange with its own shares; but, in common with a unit trust, it invests in a number of different companies. It may even spread its investments over a number of countries.

Investment trusts, like unit trusts, will also be divided between those which are most likely to produce income from the start, and those designed for capital appreciation. However, some combine both objectives.

Personal Equity Plans, often known by their initials PEP, represent a recent system of unit trust-type funds approved by the government to encourage people to invest in British enterprise.

They are offered by banks, building societies and insurance companies; the profits on the investments made in them are tax-free, and they are exempt from capital gains tax. But the amounts we are allowed to invest are limited.

Advice and Protection

Apart from professional people such as accountants, lawyers and bank managers, there are now plenty of experts ready to give us investment advice. Many of them are to be found on the High Street.

Some of them are very skilled and knowledgeable, but the important thing is to establish how independent they are and whether they are really working in our best interest. After all, they have to earn their living from somewhere. This means that it will probably come in the form of a commission, if we are not asked to pay them an adequate fee based upon a reasonable scale.

It is no good going to any adviser, if we are not ready to provide a full picture of our financial situation. We must start off by trusting them. This suggests it is a good idea to check their professional reputation before making use of them, if we do not already know them or their work. No one who is reputable will object to being asked for references, or possibly an introduction to an existing client.

Because of the growth of activity in the financial field in recent years and the relaxation in the rules over the buying and selling of stocks and shares, which can now be bought over the counter, legislation has been introduced to protect us from those who really do not know what they are doing, or who are dishonourable.

The legislation providing this protection is the Financial Services Act 1986. It resulted in the creation of a network of watchdog organizations led by the Securities and Investments Board. Before a firm can set itself up to handle our money, or to give advice, it has to be authorized.

The Act also requires financial organizations, and even consultants who work on their own, to belong to one of a number of self-regulatory bodies. Stockbrokers, too, have their own in-built system for protecting customers, if something goes wrong; so apart from the very rare, but spectacular, failures which hit the headlines, the financial system is now well monitored and investors have an effective network of protection and redress.

Names and addresses of some of the most useful organizations are:

Association of Investment Trust Companies, 16 Finsbury Circus, London EC2M 7JU, which provides booklets and list of savings schemes.

Bonds and Stocks Office, Blackpool, FY3 9YP, for government stocks and income bonds.

British Insurance and Investment Brokers Association, BIIBA House, 14 Bevis Marks, London EC3 7NT, which can give you the name and address of member firms working locally.

Building Societies Ombudsman, 35 Grosvenor Gardens, London SW1X 7AW, which is legally empowered to investigate most types of complaints.

Building Society Shop, Maid Marian Way, Nottingham, NG1 6BH, which can recommend the best buys in every type of saving scheme.

Department of National Savings, 375 Kensington High Street, London W14 8SD, for general enquiries. Current rates for national savings can be obtained from one of the following 24-hour ansaphones services: 01-605 9461, 0253- 723714, 041- 632 2766.

FIMBRA (Financial Intermediaries, Managers and Brokers Regulatory Association), 22 Great Tower Street, London EC3R 5AQ, which is the self-regulatory organization for financial intermediaries, managers and brokers.

Insurance Ombudsman Bureau, 31 Southampton Row, London WC1B 5JH, for complaints about most insurance companies.

LAUTRO (Life Assurance and Unit Trust Regulatory Organization), Centre Point, 103 New Oxford Street, London WC1A 1QH, which is the self-regulatory organization of assurance and unit trust sales.

Office of the Banking Ombudsman, 5 Fetter Lane, London EC4 1BR, for complaints against almost all the banks.

Office of Fair Trading, Breams Building, London EC4A 1PR, which examines the quality of services to consumers and publishes leaflets.

Securities and Investments Board, 3 Royal Exchange, London EC3V 3NL, which is the place to go for redress of grievances and for information.

Stock Exchange, Throgmorton Street, London EC1N 1HP, for a list of brokers for small investors and for free booklets.

Unit Trust Association, 65 Kingsway, London WC2B 6TD, which can provide a newsletter, enquiry guide and video.

Unit Trust Ombudsman, 31 Southampton Row, London WC1B 5HS, for complaints about management.

Taxation

Like it or not, we are all liable for tax in some form or other. Even if our income is small and we do not pay income tax, we do pay VAT on our purchases. The Community Charge is another form of taxation.

If we have been in employment and the tax office has dealt with our deductions through the PAYE system, we may know very little about how it works when we move to retirement. We may now have to deal directly with the Inspector of Taxes for the first time.

The best advice to give in this connection, is to remember the Inspector has his job to do. His life, as well as our own, can be made a lot easier if we are frank and open. The Inspector is not just sitting there waiting to catch us out. If we are in difficulties, or do not fully understand an aspect of the system as it affects us, it is much better to consult the Inspector rather than avoid him. He may even be able to explain about allowances we did not know we were entitled to claim.

Of course, if we have a number of different sources of income, and are perhaps involved in earning money in our retirement from a small business enterprise, or from freelance work, it is probably wise to employ an accountant. Almost certainly he or she will earn the fees we pay them in pointing out to us what claims we can properly make against our expenses.

April 6, 1990 marks a radical new departure in the taxation system. From the beginning of this particular tax year husbands and wives each take responsibility for our own taxation. This means that each of us will be taxed separately on our own income. We will have our own allowances and rate bands. We will also pay our own taxes, as well as claiming our own refunds, so there is an added reason for us to understand something about the system.

Tax-free Income

Before considering the general principles which apply to tax, it may be useful to remind ourselves which elements of our income are *tax-free*. They include:

- additional child support.

- additional pensions for holders of awards for gallantry.

- almost all gifts (although if valued at over £3,000, or if the money from the donor has not been previously taxed, there may be a liability).

- Christmas bonus.

- certain disablement pensions from the armed forces, police, or fire brigade.

- endowment policy on maturity.

- housing benefit.

- income support.

- industrial injuries benefits.

- invalidity pension.

- lump sum commuted from a pension, with an upper ceiling of £150,000.

- matured endowment policy.

- mobility allowance.

- national savings premium bond prizes.

- pensions paid to victims of Nazi oppression by Austria and West Germany.

- redundancy payment, or a golden handshake up to the value of £30,000.

- save-as-you-earn bonuses.

- short-term sickness benefits.

- war disablement benefits.

- war widows' pensions.

Calculating Our Tax Liability

Tax is payable on the following state benefits:

- invalid care allowance.

- invalidity allowance, when paid with the retirement pension.

- retirement pension.

- sick pay.

- unemployment benefit.

- widowed mother's allowance.

- widow's pension.

The amount of income tax we are liable to pay is worked out on the basis of most of our income, after the deduction of certain personal allowances. Our assessment includes our pension, the interest from all our savings, dividends, investments and from our earnings, even if these are only casual. Other taxable sources of income would be from payments made by a lodger.

There are, at present (early 1990), two rates of tax: the current basic rate of 25 per cent and the higher rate, which is 40 per cent.

Personal allowances are deducted before any calculations about the amount of tax we are liable for are made. Personal allowances are not precisely the same for everyone. Differences depend on whether we are married or single, and for married people, whether both work. There are also differences in relation to age.

The Age Allowance is an additional personal allowance, which comes in to effect when we are 65. It has been the cause of a great deal of resentment amongst women who are forced to retire, for purposes of the state pension, at 60 and who, therefore, do not receive the age allowance during the first five years of retirement.

Tax relief is also given for the first £30,000 of a mortgage paid on the purchase of our own home. This leads to the argument put forward by accountants that keeping a mortgage going is tax-efficient. However, for some people, paying off the mortgage and being free of debt is more important in terms of peace of mind.

Self-employed pension plans and personal pensions are partly exempt on a sliding scale, as well as some maintenance payments in respect of divorce and separation, and covenanted gifts (of four years or more) to charity.

The retirement pension alone is not sufficient to bring us to a point at which tax becomes due, but it is taken into account when assessing how much tax we have to pay on our income as a whole. For this reason, it has to be declared, whereas income support is not taxable.

In most cases, the investments we receive will already have had their tax deducted before the money is paid to us. For a basic rate taxpayer, there will be no further liability for tax in this respect, but for those who pay tax at the higher rate, there will be some additional liability.

Exceptions to the general rule, where the money paid to us is gross with no basic rate tax deduction, include national savings income, deposit bonds and certain types of gilt-edged securities. In these cases, both higher- and lower-rated tax payers will receive tax demands.

Capital gains tax has to be paid on profits from the sale of a major capital asset. For example, property that is not the home in which we live; stocks and shares; jewellery; works of art and other items of value.

However, there is an exemption limit of £5,000 a year, before capital gains tax becomes liable, and certain expenditure is exempt. This includes the sale of our main home; our car; personal belongings, up to the value of £3,000; the proceeds from a life assurance policy, in most circumstances; profits on government stocks, national savings certificates, save as you earn contracts, building society savings; premium bond winnings; football pool and other betting winnings; gifts to registered charities; personal equity plan schemes (PEPs). **Inheritance tax** replaced capital transfer tax, which was abolished in the 1986 Budget. The main change here was the abolition of all tax on most lifetime gifts, subject to certain conditions. These include the gift being made at least seven years before the donor's death and it must have been given unconditionally. For gifts made between three and seven years before death there is a sliding scale of taxation.

Written Information about Taxation
Your Taxes and Savings (£2.50) is published by Age Concern England (see page 128).
Your local tax office will be able to provide a series of free leaflets on different aspects of the tax system.

Making a Will

It is very important to make a will. If we do not, and we die intestate our estate (the goods and money which belonged to us) will be divided among the members of our family according to rules which are laid down by law. If we have no close family, the money will simply go to the state.

Apart from the fact that the way in which our estate is divided when we make no will may not reflect the way in which we would have wished it to be distributed, there is also a great deal of unnecessary fuss when there is no will, or when nobody knows if there is one, and where it has been put.

For all these reasons, it is worth doing the job properly in thinking about how we would like our assets distributed; whether they represent a small or a large sum, the principle is the same.

Here, again, is a situation in which *plans should be made together*. Death may not be an easy subject to discuss, but talking about it in an unemotional way, long before it is likely to happen, and keeping our affairs in a tidy way, so that at least our partner knows where to find our will and all relevant papers, is both practical and responsible.

If we make a will, we also have to decide who the executors are going to be. These are the people who have the responsibility of ensuring that our wishes are carried out and that the legal processes involved in probate are dealt with properly.

Once probate has been granted, it is then the responsibility of the executors to see that the beneficiaries, who are named in the will, receive the money or property we wish to leave to them. It is perfectly proper for a beneficiary to be an executor. Indeed, it may be a good thing to involve one in this way because s/he will want to see the administration of the estate is carried through as efficiently and quickly as possible. A second executor might be a friend who is used to dealing with official matters, or it could be a solicitor or accountant who is required to act in a professional capacity. In this case, of course, a fee will be charged.

Unless we are very rich and our financial affairs are complex, a will does not have to be a complicated document. It does not even have to be drawn up by a solicitor. We can do it for ourselves if we prefer and, in this connection, any of the following publications will be helpful:

Making a Will Won't Kill You is published by The Law Society, 113 Chancery Lane, London WC2A 1PL, and is issued free.

Wills and Probate is published and sold by the Consumers' Association. It has also produced an action-pack, *Make Your Will* (£6.95), which contains charts, forms and worksheets. Both can be obtained from the Consumers' Association, 2 Marylebone Road, London NW1 4DX.

Instructions for my next-of-kin and executors (25p) is a useful four-page form on which to fill in detailed personal financial information to help executors when the time comes for them to act. It is published by Age Concern England (see page 128).

Your local Citizens Advice Bureau or Law Centre will also be able to give you advice and information.

TWO

Somewhere To Live

When we are busily engaged in a working career, the place where we live is probably dictated by our job. In many cases, we may even have to change homes several times in response to promotion or perhaps as a result of redundancy. This means that for many of us, freedom from the pressures of work provides the first opportunity to live exactly where we would choose.

The house which suited us when we were younger and when there were children to rear, may be quite inappropriate for later life. It may be the wrong size, the wrong shape and in quite the wrong place.

What was once a source of pride and pleasure can too easily become a millstone round our neck, absorbing more money than we can afford as the battle to keep it in reasonably good shape becomes increasingly demanding on our energy, our time, and our income.

Some people solve the problem by escaping to a retirement community by the sea, in the countryside, or even on the Continent, where the constantly warm climate becomes a very attractive prospect after the damp winters we have grown accustomed to in this country. Moving, as part of a retirement plan, *can* be a tremendous success; but for many people it turns out to be a disaster, when the reasons for moving, and the kind of life the move is going to offer have not been carefully thought through beforehand.

A decision to move to a bungalow on a hill, overlooking the harbour, based on a romantic view of the future taken from the memories of a past holiday when the sun shone and the warm seas were inviting, may well turn out to be a nightmare when icy roads, biting winds, and indifferent public transport services turn our seaside castle into a prison from which there is little or no hope of escape.

For those who are lucky enough to be in a position to make a choice, there are some basic questions to be asked about our reasons for thinking about a move, as well as a number of very practical issues which need to be taken into account. All of them demand honest answers, after very careful consideration and a good deal of discussion.

Here are some of the points which need to be taken into consideration:

- is the house the right size and shape for our present needs and those we can begin to anticipate for the future?

- what about stairs? Are they likely to become an increasing problem?

- how easy is it to keep the house warm, and how expensive is its consumption of fuel? Is the system as efficient as it might be?

- is it relatively easy to maintain, or very difficult and expensive?

- what about the garden? Too big, too small or about right for the present, as well as twenty years ahead?

- how convenient are the shops and other services? One day the car will have to go.

- is it in a caring, friendly neighbourhood in which it is possible to be happy?

- is the sound of children at play a pleasure or a penance?

- will it be a wrench to move away from a network of long-standing friends and neighbours?

- how well is it placed for the closest family members who matter most?

It is worth taking plenty of time in answering these questions. None of them is simple and straightforward. But if our original response to any of them is negative, there may be something which can be done to change the situation without the need to make a move.

Two simple examples describe the possibilities. A house which we like, and which is in a neighbourhood where we feel very much at home, but which is too large, might be convertible into two flats, providing us with more manageable living space and additional income at the same time.

A garden which needs a great deal of cultivating to avoid looking like a wilderness, might be put down to grass. Or, possibly, a part of it might be let off as an allotment to someone who would welcome a plot of land, and who might in return become a valuable source of fresh vegetables!

But, here again, there are other alternatives to explore for someone who loves to work in the garden, but who may gradually begin to find it too much strain in relation to creaking joints – which are not unknown in our fifties and sixties! Flower beds can be raised, and special tools designed to help handicapped people can be bought. This prospect may seem very remote in middle age; but, without being morbid, it is sensible to consider the range of possibilities which may have to be faced over a long period of time.

But, of course, the central issue must be the house or flat itself. How many bedrooms does it have, and how many are we likely to need? Whilst it is very nice to be able to entertain friends and visitors, is it really sensible to keep two separate rooms empty for fifty weeks a year? On the other hand, retirement means that an extra person is going to be home all day. In these circumstances, an additional room, which can be converted into a workshop or a study, may become very valuable in giving both partners space in which to move.

There is never a good time to have to spend a lot of money on doing up a house; but the point of retirement, when there may be the possibility of a capital sum taken from our occupational pension, is probably as good a time as any to invest in repairs and in improving the general fabric.

Of course, the property will continue to need maintenance; but the future costs of renovation can be substantially reduced by the use of many of the modern products which are designed for long life, and which need much less care and attention than some of the traditional materials used in house building.

There will also be a number of possible sources of financial help in improving our home.

Suppose, however, that the first checklist begins to suggest that moving away to somewhere new may have attractions which outweigh staying where we are. In this case, it is worth going through another series of questions about both the advantages and disadvantages of finding somewhere new before we begin to settle on a final location. For instance, we should be considering:

- if we are thinking of moving because we want a larger, a smaller, or a more convenient home, is it best to look for somewhere in our own district, or to move right away?

- if the move is to be nearer the family, it is as well to remember they may not always stay where they are now.

- is property in the area to which we are thinking of moving more or less expensive than where we are now? This question is very important if part of the object of the move is to release some capital. Popular retirement areas are becoming much more expensive.

- what kind of environment is it? Is it flat or hilly, remembering that there will come a day when motorists become pedestrians!

- what kind of civic amenities, ranging from public transport to the library service, exist in the place to which we are thinking of moving? In this connection, it is worth making enquiries at the town hall, local Citizens Advice Bureau, or in the library itself where lists of voluntary societies and services are kept. Sometimes this information can be found in a published directory.

- what kind of community are we looking for? Somewhere which is lively and which has plenty of social, cultural, sporting or educational activities in which to join, or somewhere very quiet and relatively undeveloped where people have to be pretty self-reliant and prefer to keep themselves to themselves?

- if we are a member of a church or a religious community, do we know if it is active where we are thinking of going to live?

- if it is a seaside resort in which we are interested, have we taken into account the fact they are sometimes too full of life in the summer, and much too quiet in the winter when everyone has deserted them? Walking along a blustery promenade in a force nine gale may lose its attraction after a while.

- what kind of health and social services does the area have?

As with all the other series of questions posed in this book, the really important ones to ask are those which we list for ourselves; but if we put the questions, we must also give ourselves honest answers. Cheating will get us nowhere or, perhaps worse still, it will lead us to choose to move in quite the wrong direction.

Here again, plans have to be made on the basis of the preferences of both partners. After all, one of us in a marriage is going to outlive the other. A remote idyllic spot is going to be a misery if the survivor cannot drive the car, is unable to get around and has few, if any, close friends.

But if a serious and well thought-out decision about moving seems to be emerging, it is very important to make a number of visits to the chosen spot, in bad weather as well as in good. It is also well worthwhile asking people who already live there what they feel about the place. Do not rely on the glowing language of the estate agent's glossy brochure, or of the description of life in the neighbourhood by the vendor of a property which looks suitable at first sight!

It is also important to look over the top of garden hedges and fences to see what is on the other side of a property in which we may be interested. A primary school at the end of the garden with two hundred children pouring out into the playground three times a day, may not be the ideal spot for a restful retirement home. But there will be no reference to it in the sales literature.

It is worthwhile making visits during both weekends and weekdays. The noise of traffic may be markedly different on Wednesdays and Sundays.

Although, in theory, it is always possible to put right a mistaken move, the reality in making a second one, or even of returning to the place in which we had lived before, can become an expensive and a frustrating business, which is far better avoided.

Another question which must be asked about any retirement community is related to the atmosphere of a neighbourhood where most people are from the same generation. This can have its advantages, with no late night parties and a general responsiveness to the needs of older customers in the shops; but, for some people, there is an attraction in living in a mixed community.

Retirement towns in America have proved very popular, and a number of villages are being developed in this country, but they are, by no means, everyone's choice. They must be thought about very carefully from every angle.

Moving Overseas

The importance of getting it right is even more crucial with a move overseas.

Being forced to give up a retirement villa in Spain, in quite late life when many connections have been severed, may turn out to be a difficult and sad business. Here, it is even more important to delay a purchase until a thorough visit of exploration has been made.

The brochures make it all look so easy and attractive. The promotional visits are very alluring and the salesman's answers to any of our questions are reassuring. For those who pick the right place, and are blessed with good health, it may turn out to be the fulfilment of a dream but there must be good reasons for the trail of unsatisfied villa owners coming back to start life all over again, after what may well have been an expensive lesson.

It is even more important to explore the area very thoroughly when thinking about moving abroad, as well as studying the weather chart for the whole year round. It is much more than simply finding the right home in an attractive area.

It is also well worth finding out the snags, as well as the benefits, from people who already have established themselves. One of the most important facts to discover is the standard of health care and which services are available on what terms. For example, will an English health care insurance policy be acceptable?

If we decide to make the move, and can afford to keep even a small home in this country, it will provide a base for visits, so that we do not lose touch altogether, and a place to return to if it becomes necessary in later life. It may also provide a source of income through letting.

There are other matters to be considered about moving abroad. Differences in language, law, and customs all have a bearing on the quality of life for an expatriate. The tax regulations about status and nationality are also complicated. They need to be studied carefully. They are described in a booklet, well worth reading, produced by the Inland Revenue. It is *IR20: Residents' and Non-residents' liability to Tax in the UK*, and may be obtained from tax offices.

Staying Put

If, on reflection, we decide it is better to stay where we are, it is worth considering ways of making use of the financial value of our home. There are now a number of schemes which are proving increasingly attractive to older home owners.

Firstly, there is the possibility of an *interest only mortgage*. The obvious disadvantage of a loan of this kind is that the debt will never be discharged, and the amount of money we will have to leave will be reduced; the advantage is that the re-payments are much lower when we are only required to pay the interest, but not pay back the capital. Building societies and banks, as well as some other financial institutions, now make these loans. Their rates of interest may vary so it is worth shopping around for the best terms. There will also be an upper limit on the amount which can be borrowed.

Other schemes, known as *home reversion* schemes, have been developed in which it is possible to sell all, or part, of our house at a substantial discount, while retaining the right to re-main in it for the rest of our life at a nominal rent. The pro-ceeds from the sale can then be used to purchase an annuity and to provide a guaranteed income.

These schemes seem outwardly attractive, but they have their disadvantages: the amount paid for the property may be no more than 50 per cent of its market value; we will not bene-fit from future increases in property value on our house; it becomes very difficult to move, because we no longer have access to the original capital; and, of course, the home can no longer be left to our beneficiaries.

Some reversionary schemes now make it possible for the home owner to obtain a capital sum for part of the value of the house, with a transfer of partial ownership to the company running the scheme.

Anyone contemplating the use of one of these schemes would be well advised to discuss the implications with a solicitor and make sure they fully understand them before going ahead.

Publications which could also be helpful here are:

Raising an Income from your Home, (free, but enclose a stamped addressed envelope) and **Your Home as Capital** (£1.95), both from Age Concern England (see page 128).

Extra Income for Life for Elderly Houseowners is available free from Hinton and Wild (Home Plans) Ltd, Freepost, Surbiton, Surrey KT6 7BR.

Bungalows and Flats

For those of us who may have lived our whole life in a house, the idea of a bungalow or a flat may not appeal. On the other hand, living on one floor has increasing attractions in later life when the available space is more concentrated, stairs are no longer necessary and, in the case of a flat, when there may be services provided.

Another advantage of a flat is the possibility of leaving it for a while, perhaps during a winter holiday, and knowing it will be looked after, with less risk of burst pipes or unwelcome intruders.

But if we have not experienced life in a flat before, it is very important to be quite clear about the actual arrangements for care and maintenance, as well as for any common services such as central heating, which may be provided with the lease and for which we will have to pay. This applies as much to a purpose-built block of flats as it does to a conversion of a single house into two or three living units. Service charges vary enormously, and it is important to know what they include. One way of finding out is to ask for the management accounts for recent years.

Whilst flats may provide a sense of security; their disadvantage may lie in the restrictions which go with having to share a building with other people as well as with their noises!

Bungalows may offer a greater sense of freedom and they are likely to offer a garden; but some people may feel more vulnerable on the ground floor if going to bed has always meant going upstairs; so here again it is important to explore the situation very thoroughly before making a break with what may have been the habits of a lifetime.

Mobile Homes

Mobile homes were originally large caravans on permanent sites. Now they are much more sophisticated. They may look to all intents and purposes very much like small bungalows.

They come as a ready-made package with curtains, carpets and most fittings and are very easy to maintain. They are quite expensive, however, and their value depreciates, whereas the value of a traditional house almost certainly increases. There may come a time when they have to be replaced, with little or no return on the original investment.

Building societies will not offer mortgages on mobile homes, although site owners often have arrangements for obtaining financial loans where the interest can be off-set against tax.

The site operator will charge fees and may include re-sale restrictions, which it is essential to be clear about before purchasing a mobile home. The site owner will also be entitled to a commission on any sales.

Sharing Homes

Sharing a home may not seem like a very attractive proposition to many, but it is one way of ensuring companionship and an additional income in later life.

If the home is shared between an older person who is a grandparent, or who can assume a surrogate role as one, it may bring a sense of purpose and meaning into the relationship for both generations; but, of course, any arrangement of this nature needs to be thought about very carefully before-hand. It should never be entered into on a permanent basis until there is reasonable certainty it is going to work. The person who may be giving up a home should not let go entirely, until there is real confidence about the long-term future.

Apart from the personalities of the people involved, sharing a home also depends upon the physical arrangements of the house. If there is not adequate private space for everyone the arrangement will probably be doomed from the start.

If the house is large enough for an adaptation, then what has become known as a 'granny annex' may represent the most successful compromise, because both the young family and those who are older can really enjoy a combination of privacy and proximity.

Anyone thinking about the possibility of adapting a home in this way to provide two living units must remember that both planning permission and building regulations may be involved.

Even though most arrangements for living together within the family circle are probably made informally, it is well worthwhile checking on the rights of a landlord or tenant, depending upon who is moving into whose house. Things can go wrong, and it is much better to start the relationship on the basis of a very clear understanding about who is responsible for what, and about any financial arrangements for sharing the costs of certain items.

Of course, sharing a home can also be arranged with a friend. Here professional advice about the basis of the arrangement is even more important than within the family, especially if a joint purchase is being contemplated.

Tenants

Unfortunately, many of the choices open to the increasing number of house-owners are not available to tenants of private landlords or of local councils.

There is a national mobility scheme, to which most housing

authorities belong, in order to help tenants move from one area to another. It is not necessary to be a council house tenant to be considered; but the council would have to approve an application to place anyone on the list.

The first step to take is to go to the council's housing department and ask for details. The local Citizens Advice Bureau will have an explanatory leaflet about the scheme.

Some people succeed in advertising the potential availability of the home they want to change in the areas to which they hope to move. There is a private exchange bureau called Locatex which offers to assist council and housing association tenants who want to move, but exchanges are quite few and far between. The Locatex Bureau address is PO Box 1, March, Cambridgeshire PE15 8HJ.

One of the most likely possibilities for a move on the part of older tenants, is through a housing association. There are about 2,600 associations in the country providing a range of specialized accommodation. Many concentrate on the provision of sheltered housing to rent; but in most cases, their waiting lists are quite long. This means making plans as early as possible.

Converting the Home

If improvements are necessary, or desirable, in making our home more comfortable and convenient for later life, it is very important to deal with a reputable builder and to pay serious attention to the seven golden rules produced by the Office of Fair Trading. They are:

■ before you start – decide exactly what you want done. For larger jobs get advice from an architect or a surveyor.

■ ask at the Planning Department of your local council whether you need planning permission or building regulations approval: this is especially important if your house is in a conservation area, is a 'listed building', or if the work involves changing the frontage.

- the Planning Department will also be able to tell you whether you can get a grant towards the work.

- get estimates and quotations in writing from at least two firms. Find out as much as you can about them.

- make sure that your contract is in writing and gives full details of prices, cancellation rights, guarantees and when the work will be started and finished. Check whether any sub-contractors are to be used and who is liable if things go wrong.

- be careful about parting with money in advance, especially if you are asked to pay large deposits. Always query any price increases and ask why they were not included in the original estimate.

- if you have a problem, act quickly and get advice from the Trading Standards (or Consumer Protection) department of your local council or the Citizens Advice Bureau.

A number of schemes, usually called either *Care and Repair* or *Staying Put,* have been designed for older people with a limited income. They exist to help with the actual process of getting work done in the house and are organized by voluntary organizations or housing associations. They will arrange surveys; find builders; supervise the work whilst it is being carried out; explore sources of finance; and liaise with the Department of Social Security, where this is appropriate. Unfortunately, these schemes are not available everywhere. On the whole, they are not council run, nor are they nationwide. They are often run by voluntary housing associations. Enquire at local Citizens Advice Bureaux or housing departments.

A 'Gifted Housing Scheme', run by Help the Aged (see page 128), involves donating our house to the charity which will then convert it into one or more units, depending upon its size. After the conversion is complete, we can return to live there with none of the responsibilities of ownership.

Some housing associations also have schemes in which we can sell them our home, on the understanding we stay in it for the rest of our life. The money from the sale will provide immediate capital for repairs and improvements. But housing associations are not in a position to pay the full market price and the house will not be included in our estate, since it is no longer in our ownership.

Sources of financial help with repairs

Home improvement grants are provided by local councils. They cover a proportion of the costs of certain types of repair and improvement, if the age and condition of the property meet certain conditions.

However, a combination of severe government cuts in spending and heavy demand for grants in recent years, has resulted in long waiting lists in some areas. Where this is the case, the only grants awarded may be for the provision of basic amenities.

Grants fall under three main headings to cover different types of work:

■ intermediate grants are awarded towards the cost of amenities which are missing altogether, for example, an inside lavatory, bath, or hot and cold water supply. They do not cover central heating. These amenities are mandatory so the council must provide them. To qualify, the house or flat in question must have been built before 1961.

■ improvement grants are for major repair work. Central heating can be covered if it is part of a major improvement to a property, built before 1961, which has a rateable value of less than £225 (or £400 if it is in London). These grants are discretionary. For someone living in a Housing Action Area (or Housing Renewal Area), or who is disabled, the limits do not apply. (Enquire from the local council whether yours is a designated Housing Renewal Area.)

■ repairs grants are available towards the cost of major structural repairs to properties built before 1919. The replacement of worn-out fixtures is not included, nor is routine maintenance. Rewiring can only be grant-aided if it is part of a large programme of work. Conditions about property values are the same as for improvement grants, and these grants are also discretionary.

The amounts of grants awarded will vary quite considerably, but they will normally be between 50 and 70 per cent of the total approved cost – unless the applicant is considered to be a priority case, in which case the grant may be higher. (Grants are affected by the amount central government invests, but since 1983, when there was a very heavy spending programme, they have been considerably reduced.)

A golden rule with any of these grants is that the work must never be started before an application is approved.

In addition to the general grants available from the public purse, there are certain additional sources of help for disabled people. These are normally given a high priority. They may be awarded in the following circumstances:

■ to provide extra standard amenities, if the existing ones cannot be reached, or used, by a disabled occupant.

■ improvement grants for adaptation to make it possible for a disabled person to use the home, for example, installing a downstairs bathroom or lavatory, putting in a stair lift or providing a ramp for a wheelchair. Alterations in bathrooms and kitchens are also covered, and so is electrical work to make switches and sockets accessible.

■ both the intermediate and improvement grants for disabled people qualify for higher eligible expense limits and grant rates. Also, the property in question does not have to have been built before 1961 and the rateable value limits do not apply.

In most cases, the award of a grant will involve the endorsement of an occupational therapist who will be required to confirm that the work is necessary. The therapist will be employed by the local social services authority which will be involved in the application, together with the housing and/or environmental health department.

Under the terms of the 1970 Chronically Sick and Disabled Persons Act, local authority social service departments have a duty to assist in making arrangements for adaptations. This includes providing financial assistance and helping with an assessment of what work is needed, as well as in having plans prepared and liaising with other council departments which may have an interest in the matter.

Social service authorities also have a duty to help with necessary adaptations which are not covered by home improvement grants as well as with the provision of additional facilities designed to make the property more safe, more comfortable and more convenient.

Unfortunately, there are considerable differences between one local authority and another in implementing this act. This means the amount of help which may be made available will depend upon the priorities and finances of the council in whose area we live.

■ Insulation grants are available towards the cost of insulating lofts and lagging hot water tanks and pipes. Cold water tanks which are in the loft also qualify. For someone in receipt of income support or community charge benefit, a grant of up to 90 per cent of the cost can be awarded with a maximum of £144; otherwise, no grant is available. As with all other improvement grants, approval must be sought before the work begins.

Apart from these grants from statutory sources, for those who qualify, there are other ways in which we may be able to raise loans. Sources include building societies, which will sometimes give unsecured loans for small amounts, although the interest rate will be higher than for a normal mortgage. Banks provide loans, which are not cheap; but loans from finance companies will be very expensive with extremely high interest rates and they are best avoided, if at all possible.

Some useful publications and sources of help are:

Paying for Repairs and Improvements to Your Home, issued by the Department of the Environment and available free from councils and advice centres.

Home Improvement Grants, a publication issued by the Department of the Environment and available free from local councils and advice centres.

Housing Options for Older People (£2.50), **Owning Your House in Retirement** (£1.50) and **Using Your Home as Capital** (£2.50), all available from Age Concern England (see page 128).

Home Safety

We are all becoming more conscious of the need to make our homes and streets more secure. And it is certainly better to be safe than sorry.

Outer security

Although the statistics confirm that older people are less vulnerable to physical attacks than young people in the street, with increasing age and less acute sight and hearing it is important to ensure that sensible precautions are taken at home to provide a genuine sense of security against intruders, as well as to reduce the risk of accidents.

The police suggest that nine out of ten break-ins happen because of insecure doors and windows and many of them could have been prevented with a little forethought and at no great expense. As far as protection against intruders is concerned, it is certainly sensible to invite the local Crime Prevention Officer from the Police to call and advise on the best way of making the home secure.

Door chains and good locks, which comply with official

British standards (look for the BSI kite mark), can be bought from most ironmongers or do-it-yourself stores. Patio doors and glass-panelled doors should have specially designed locks. Strong bolts at the top and bottom of outside doors provide an added protection.

Windows with simple latches which can be easily lifted are no deterrent to the burglar looking for opportunities to slip into our home and louvered windows present an open invitation to the uninvited guest. Security window locks can make a considerable improvement.

If there is no way of seeing who is at the door, a door viewer can be a very useful source of early warning and protection.

None of these precautionary measures need cost much to buy or install. The more sophisticated burglar alarms can be quite expensive, although the price is probably worth paying if it brings peace of mind. However, a dog may be just as effective and a good deal more pleasant to have around the house! At least one insurance company offers a lower premium to owners of small noisy dogs.

Safety inside the house
Safety in the home can be greatly improved by checking that the electric system has been renewed in an old house, that passages and stairs are well lit, and that frayed old carpets are replaced. Among the most frequent accidents in later life are those which occur on the stairs. They can bring considerable pain and discomfort with broken hips which then have to be repaired with surgery for which there can be long waits. It is much better to deal with these matters at the beginning of retirement than leaving them until later.

It is probably also wise to install smoke alarms, certainly in the kitchen. They are easy to fit and they are cheap.

There is a growing market in personal alarm systems worn by older people, which undoubtedly give a sense of security and they may well be the means of summoning help in a crisis, but the personal interest of neighbours remains the most important source of continuing personal contact and the most immediate source of help in time of trouble.

Meeting Special Needs

Although most of us naturally hope to end our days in our own home, for some people a degree of support becomes necessary as they grow older. This may be provided by sheltered housing where those living there continue to have their own front door. There are also residential and nursing homes which, at their best, combine security, care and privacy.

Sheltered Housing

Sheltered housing, as we now know it, in terms of independent living, with its own in-built support system was first introduced by local authorities and housing associations more than thirty years ago.

In recent years, commercial property developers have also recognized the growing market in retirement homes, and estates are being built all over the country. In some cases, they are simply a complex of small, easy-to-run houses or flats, which would be just as suitable for young couples as they are for those who are older.

But the commercial market has also witnessed a considerable development in sheltered housing, which has been seen by many people as the best solution to living in old age. Although sheltered housing is being presented as if it were a modern solution to the living needs of older people, it is not a new idea at all.

The medieval almshouses, built by our Elizabethan forbears, were actually an ideal form of sheltered housing. They were designed to give their occupiers the dignity and privacy of having their own front door, and of living an independent life with support on hand when it was needed. They were also often very beautiful buildings.

But the old almshouses often had other advantages over modern schemes because they were built in the centre of their communities next to the village green, the church, the shop and the pub. Unfortunately, the same cannot always be said about many modern sheltered housing schemes. They are often neither very convenient nor beautiful, and descriptions about their situation near shops and all conveniences need to be taken with a pinch of salt since they are often about as realistic as the flights of fancy of those holiday brochures which wax lyrical about sea views and access to the beach.

However, sheltered housing schemes, wherever situated, do provide accommodation with independence up to a point. They may be designed to encourage continued mobility, as their occupiers become older, and there will be a warden on hand to respond to crisis calls and keep a general eye on things. Internal communication systems should ensure that messages for help can be heard immediately; but, except in very limited schemes, sheltered housing is not designed to provide a home for its residents when a considerable amount of care and support becomes needed. At this point they may have to move on. Research has confirmed that very old and frail people probably manage better and for longer in their original homes with familiar surroundings.

However, there is now a move by some enlightened local authorities, housing associations and private companies to develop what is becoming known as *very sheltered housing,* which really falls halfway between sheltered housing and residential care.

Such housing has a system of additional support built into it. For example, there may be a restaurant where daily lunches can be taken. There may be additional domestic support available to individual owners or tenants so that they can cope with quite considerable degrees of disability.

The design of homes within the scheme will also take into account the possible need for a wheel-chair, and baths may be converted into shower-rooms. The approach is to make it possible to bring essential services to the people, rather than to make people move towards the services.

Some sheltered housing schemes go some way towards an integrated system by having extra care units attached to them, or run within the same organization; but the idea which was commonly held twenty years ago – that people could be neatly divided into the active elderly population, the elderly population in need of a sheltered environment, and those who required residential care – has now been exploded.

The reality is that most of us prefer to remain in our own homes for as long as possible, and the average age in which a move is made to special housing or residential care, grows higher each year, so the need for an in-built support system has become much more important.

This means that very careful thought needs to be given to a possible move towards sheltered housing, about the length of time it will be appropriate, and whether the services provided are really going to be adequate in the years ahead.

There are also questions to be answered about the basis of charging for whatever services are going to be made available, and the terms on which they are offered. As a result, a code of practice has been agreed by representatives of the commercial sector to which all new schemes must comply if they are to be registered with the National House Builders Council. Without this registration, the accommodation for sale may not attract building society mortgages.

The code requires protection for the residents to be enshrined in a management agreement between the builder and the management organization responsible for selling and administering the scheme. All schemes built after April 1990 should adhere to the code; but some builders had already adopted it before this date.

Under the terms of the code, every purchaser must be given an information pack when paying the deposit. It will include the following information:

- the names of the developer and management organization, and a statement of the relationship between them.

- the purchaser's legal rights.

- a detailed breakdown of services and service charges.

- a clear statement of the repairs and maintenance responsibilities of the manager and the resident.

- the warden's role and the required performance of the alarm system.

- the consultation and complaints procedures.

- re-sale arrangements, restrictions and charges.

A condition described in this package to study most carefully is that which outlines the basis of service charges. What elements do they include and what arrangements are made for their payment? The information should include a precise description of the services being provided; how the charge is calculated and paid; how much it is, and what are the rights of residents to query the charge and challenge it.

There are a number of different ways in which sheltered housing is sold. Mostly, it is marketed at full value, and the purchaser gets back full value when selling it, less any restrictions and charges which the purchaser's information pack must make clear.

Some councils, and a few housing associations, have schemes in which it is possible to purchase a share of the sheltered housing unit and pay rent on the remainder.

Leasehold schemes for elderly people which are run by housing associations, involve a purchase of 70 per cent of the lease, with a subsidy for the remaining share being funded by the government. When the purchaser leaves the scheme, 70 per cent of the property's market value at the time of the sale will be returned.

A few organizations, mainly charities, provide sheltered housing on a loan stock, or licence basis. In this case, the purchaser makes an interest-free loan to the organization for the housing unit. When leaving, the sum originally put in will be returned without interest. In these schemes, the amount of the loan should be a good deal less than the market price would have been; but there will also be service charges and other costs.

Some developers offer to sell units at a percentage of the full purchase price but, by the same token, only a percentage of the sale price will be received at the end.

Another scheme introduced by developers is an option to purchase a 'life-share'. This is arranged through a finance company at a percentage of the asking price. It buys the right to live in the property for life, after which the whole value of the property passes to the property company. It is also possible to purchase a half share in this way.

All these variations need careful examination, and it is best to take professional advice about the small print in agreements which will restrict rights to ownership in any way.

In many ways, a straightforward mortgage for someone who is young enough, or an interest-only mortgage in later life, may prove to be the most attractive way of funding the purchase of a unit of sheltered housing. As things stand at the moment, help with payment of the interest may be available for anyone in receipt of income support.

You may obtain names and addresses from the local Citizens Advice Bureau or the National Federation of Housing Associations, 175 Grays Inn Road, London WC1X 8UP.

Residential Care

For some people there comes a time when it is best to move into residential care. The prospect is usually not pleasing because it is regarded as a point of no return. It need not be like this, and some people may find a period in a residential setting provides the necessary rest and revitalization to return to the wider community again afterwards. What is known as 'respite care' is increasingly being seen as a way of giving both the older person and their family, or those who are caring for them, a break.

However, for some people having the household chores undertaken by someone else comes as a blessed relief, after years of being tied to the kitchen. Living in a residential home, with this freedom from domestic responsibilities, may provide the opportunity to spend time reading or painting, or pursuing hobbies for which there has been little or no time before.

Residential homes which may be run by local authorities, voluntary agencies, or commercial proprietors, are increasingly subject to inspection and to the provision of decent standards of privacy and care.

A number of homes run by charities are associated with a particular profession or trade association. For someone who retains an interest in a working career and the people with whom it was associated, a home which will bring regular contact with other like-minded people may provide an additional interest. The disadvantage of these specialist homes is the fact that they are relatively few and far between, so it may not be possible to find a place close at hand. Other homes which cater for affinity groups are provided by church-orientated bodies.

In no circumstances should anyone stay in a privately run home which is not registered with the local authority. It is also sensible to try an experimental period of perhaps a month to find out if the place is liked and it is possible to be comfortable and happy in it. This applies whether the home is run by a private owner or by a voluntary agency. In far too many cases, older people have been hurried into homes and their own property disposed of before they were certain the move was right for them and they had found somewhere to settle.

The charges for residential care vary very widely, and for residents who are not in receipt of income support, it is important to consider the size of available capital in relation to the charges which will have to be met for a considerable period of time. Once capital runs out, the costs of residential care can be met through social security, but the amount provided will certainly not meet the high fees often charged.

THREE

Leisure For Pleasure

The dictionary defines leisure as 'time at one's disposal'. Time to fill or time to kill. Relaxation is an art which has to be understood to be enjoyed. It takes many forms. At one end of the scale it may be manifest in feverish activity; at the other in soporific idleness. Each can be absorbing and pleasant at the right time and place because we can *re*-create ourselves by activity as well as by rest.

Contentment is a state of mind and so is boredom; they are both largely self-made. In this respect we are free agents and in retirement more free than ever.

Leisure should be seen as the prize of retirement and the reward for a hard-working career. The battle for its achievement will only have been won if it is associated with a genuine sense of personal fulfilment. It is also to be shared in retirement. Whilst each of us in a long-standing relationship will have our own interests which we want to pursue, it is important that some of our new activities should be explored jointly with our partner.

The great increase in amenities, including many of the new leisure centres we now have in this country, make it possible for anyone to engage in pursuits which were once limited to a privileged minority. There is no excuse for not trying something which looks interesting. The barriers really have come down, and it is not necessary to go on an expedition to the Himalayas in order to climb a mountain; to own a yacht in order to spend the summer months messing about in a boat; or to have an honours degree in history to be able to dig for the ruins of an ancient Roman villa.

Magnificent recorded music can be borrowed from most public libraries, and a course on painting, bee-keeping or astronomy can be taken for a very small fee. It is really all there on our doorstep – or, at least, on radio and television. The art is knowing what would interest us and how to set about finding it. It is also important to have some confidence. We should not be frightened of launching into something new, or perhaps of returning to the classroom after thirty or forty years. There is no disgrace in learning at our own pace.

Of course, some people will want to continue with some form of paid work in retirement, either because it provides the most interesting prospect, or because the additional income it can generate is important. Opportunities in this direction, as well as a few hints about starting up an enterprise of our own are described on pages 103-110.

First, we explore three aspects in the creative use of leisure – voluntary service for the benefit of the community; recreation through education; hobbies and physical recreation. Of course, in some cases it is possible to combine all three. They are certainly not mutually exclusive. The Red Cross or St John Ambulance Brigade volunteer at a sporting event, for instance, is giving skilled service, after detailed study of the theory and practice of first aid, whilst being entertained at the same time. The grandfather whose hobby is military history and who takes his grandsons on a sightseeing tour of a castle or an old battlefield is also serving a number of purposes at the same time. So is a retired farmer teaching modern agricultural methods as a volunteer in an African village.

Voluntary Work and the Community

Voluntary service offers a practical way of being a good neighbour for anyone who is prepared to offer time and talents for the benefit of others. There is no reason why it should not also provide us with a sense of pleasure and satisfaction.

83

Voluntary service is not a substitute for responsibilities which should be taken by public authorities, although if policies of community care are going to become a reality, there will need to be a genuine sense of partnership. However, it is one of the features of active citizenship on which a decent society depends. Its basic ingredients are compassion and common sense, together with time to spare, and a commitment to honour the promises we make about turning up where and when we are wanted. This is not to say that spontaneous acts of kindness performed over the garden fence are not just as valuable.

Whilst it is perfectly reasonable for volunteers to find the work absorbing, it would be wrong to use it simply as a means of indulging in curiosity about other people's problems or of working something troublesome out of our own system. Nor should it be regarded as a form of 'do-gooding'. Volunteers have just as much to gain as to give.

Not all voluntary jobs involve close personal relationships. There are equally important but less demanding jobs such as delivering meals, taking books around hospital wards or helping to run activities in a social club. Here what is needed is a cheerful disposition and the ability to get on friendly terms with all sorts of people. On the other hand, the voluntary visitor who is going to spend time in the homes of lonely old people must be able to draw out their interests. After all, it is not much use spending time with someone if we have nothing in common to talk about.

At the other end of the scale, there is a whole range of jobs to be done behind the scenes. Whether we are natural organizers and want responsibility, or are shy and retiring, there is bound to be something useful which we can do in the office of a charity or, in some cases, from our own home. Voluntary organizations also need people who enjoy fund-raising and have an aptitude for it.

In recent years an increasing consciousness about the importance of the environment has opened up a whole range of possibilities for voluntary service out-of-doors. These include reclaiming wasteland, establishing rights of way, opening up canals and generally improving parks and woodlands, many of which were badly damaged in the great storm of 1987. There has been a considerable growth in the number and scope of conservation bodies, all of which are grateful for people who will give time to their work in acting as wardens and guides, or in undertaking physical tasks. Many of these schemes are based on group work and provide an ideal means of bringing younger and older people together while making a practical contribution to the preservation of our common heritage.

We can choose to find a task which makes use of our existing knowledge and experience or, in retirement, we may want to do something which is entirely unrelated to our previous occupation. Sticking envelopes or keeping records may seem less spectacular than running a playgroup or a car pool, but they are just as important.

The one condition we must accept is that, having decided to become a volunteer and take on a job, we are in honour bound to turn up when we have promised. That is why it is probably better to start by doing a little and then building up if we find it suits us. There is nothing worse than a volunteer who takes on too much to begin with in an unrealistic burst of enthusiasm and then does not keep it up.

Some voluntary jobs involve selection and training – for example, marriage guidance counselling, working with the telephone Samaritans or in a Citizens Advice Bureau. In these cases the process is designed to transform the well-intentioned volunteer into one who is also well-informed. It is really no good starting out to give someone else information or even advice if we do not have a pretty clear knowledge of what we are talking about or at least where the information can be found. In some cases a selection process is involved and here it is important not to feel rejected if we are not considered suitable for the particular task which seemed to interest us. There are always plenty more!

A very useful starting point in many towns and cities will be a volunteer bureau. This is where a register of all the different kinds of jobs on offer in the local community will be kept. In a way, it is really rather like a labour exchange with descriptions of the time the work has to be undertaken, the expenses which can be met (and this may be important in retirement), what the jobs actually involve and whether training or preparation is given. There will also be a list of groups which are very informal, as well as those which may involve wearing a uniform, or some form of identification.

Before looking around to find out what needs to be done, it is important to ask ourselves some questions about our interests and strengths, as well as our limitations and prejudices. After all, if we cannot stand the sight of blood, it is not much use volunteering for an emergency rescue service!

Some of the questions to ask include:

■ do we get on well with people and make relationships easily, or are we rather shy and retiring?

■ do we like working with other people, or prefer to do things on our own?

■ are we good listeners?

■ do we expect voluntary service to be 'rewarding' and to see immediate results for what we do?

■ do we hope to resolve some of our own problems by involving ourselves in other people's lives?

■ have we been through some painful experience, or illness perhaps, which we are ready to share with others in a similar situation?

■ how well do we get on with very young children, teenagers, old people?

■ are we at ease when we are with people who suffer from

a physical or mental handicap?

■ does eccentric behaviour provoke compassion, amusement or revulsion?

■ does anger about anti-social acts outweigh our sympathy for the offender?

■ what are our practical skills?

■ do we want to use our existing experience, or find something quite new?

■ do we want to lead or to follow?

■ are we strong enough to do physical work – for example, lifting people who may be quite heavy?

■ do we have a car, and are we prepared to use it?

■ how much time can we really spare on a regular basis?

By going through this list, and asking other questions of ourself, we can begin to build up a picture of the kind of work we might find interesting and, equally important, what we should avoid at all costs.

There is no need to feel guilty if, on reflection, we doubt if we would feel comfortable with people who have to cope with particular disabilities. It is better for their sake, and our own, not to feel a sense of duty which may lead us into situations where everyone feels uncomfortable and ill-at-ease.

The list of voluntary societies, both large and small, national and local, is so long that it is almost impossible to believe there are not a number which would be able to offer us the kind of work we should like to do in company with people whom we would find congenial.

Apart from the volunteer bureaux, most public libraries or Citizens Advice Bureaux will have lists of what is happening locally. There is also a national service called REACH (Retired Executives Action Clearing House – see page 88), which sets out to match up retired people with known experience in business or management with charities which urgently need the skills they have to offer, but cannot afford to pay them. This idea has proved quite attractive to numbers of senior people who relished the challenge of taking on a new task in a totally different setting from the ones they were used to.

Community Service Volunteers (see below), which originally came into being to recruit young people to give service, between leaving school and going on to further education, now also runs a scheme called Retired and Senior Volunteer Programme (RSVP). This is designed to recruit volunteers who are over 50 and who want to become involved in community work.

Some Useful Addresses
The National Association of Volunteer Bureaux, St Peter's College, College Road, Satley, Birmingham B8 3TE, can give addresses of local bureaux.
The Volunteer Centre, 29 Lower King's Road, Berkhamstead, Hertfordshire HP4 2AB, runs courses and publishes useful material about volunteering.
Retired Executives Action Clearing House (REACH), 89 Southwark Street, London SE1 OHD.
Community Service Volunteers, 237 Pentonville Road, London N1 9NJ.

Giving Voluntary Service Overseas

Voluntary service overseas is also becoming an attractive proposition for numbers of retired people who feel they have the time and energy to go abroad for a period. One organization called British Executive Service Overseas (see page 89), which was started by the Institute of Directors, works with support from the government in providing consultants with management, professional, or technical expertise to help in the third world. Assignments usually last from between two to six months, and volunteers can also take their partners, with air fares and living costs met.

Several of the well-known voluntary agencies which send young volunteers into the third world are now beginning to recruit older volunteers, at the end of a working career, rather than at its beginning, to work overseas. But in this case, the assignments will last for a much longer period, perhaps two years. In some cases married couples can go out and work together, as long as both partners have skills which are needed.

The addresses of organizations looking for older volunteers to go overseas are:

British Executive Service Overseas, 10 Belgrave Square, London SW1X 8PH.

International Voluntary Service, Ceresole House, 53 Regent Road, Leicester LE1 6YL.

The Catholic Institute for International Relations, 22 Coleman Fields, London N1 7AF.

The United Nations Association, 3 Whitehall Court, London SW1 2EL.

Voluntary Service Overseas, 317 Putney Bridge Road, London SW15 2PN.

Learning in Later Life

The idea that people find it difficult to acquire new knowledge in middle age onwards just is not true. An experiment conducted some years ago in Australia, in which a class of schoolchildren and a group of pensioners went into a language laboratory together to study the same course, resulted in quicker initial absorption by the young people, but when they were tested a year later, the young people had forgotten a great deal which the older people remembered.

Apart from the quality of the teaching itself, learning is partly to do with aptitude and partly with motivation. If we are sufficiently interested in something, we are much more likely to succeed: learning Greek, in preparation for a holiday visit to Athens, may well be more likely to absorb us than if we had to study it simply because it was on the curriculum without any immediate relevance. True scholars, who delight in learning for its own sake, are few and far between.

There has been a long tradition of adult education in this country. It was originally designed to compensate for lost learning in childhood and was provided by voluntary societies like the Adult School Union and the Workers' Educational Association, as well as by university extra-mural departments and by local education authorities, which are now the major providers. Other groups, such as the Women's Institute movement, have also included adult learning as a central part of their work, and many countrywomen have good reason to be grateful for the lessons they have learnt at the WI.

In the past few years, there has also been a rapid development in 'distance learning', through correspondence schools, the BBC and Open University. These networks have provided direct access to diploma and degree courses for people who would otherwise never have considered re-entering a classroom. They have opened up learning possibilities for all of us.

They combine home study with personal tuition. Apart from the *range* of courses they offer, they also *allow us to study at our own pace*. This comes as a great relief to many people, after thirty years away from the classroom and the discipline of the formal learning process.

In thinking about education in later life, it is helpful to consider it under three quite distinct headings.

First, the essentially *practical approach,* chiefly concerned with instruction, information, and perhaps the development of new interests or hobbies, for example, indoor gardening, continental cookery or motor maintenance. Learning something new in this context may involve the use of newspapers, radio, television, or journals, as well as organized classes, and what might be described as activity groups.

The second approach consists of courses which may lead to a certificate or award of attendance, and which *demand more*

90

sustained study with background reading. The third approach is the purely academic one of *full university courses* offering diplomas or degrees.

Before considering which kind of course and which setting would suit us best, there are questions to be answered:

- is it to up-date skills, such as typing, which already exist?

- is it to return to study which was cut short years ago?

- does a course need to have a very practical orientation – upholstery, cookery or car maintenance, for example?

- is part of the object of taking up a class the opportunity it offers to meet new people? If this is the case, a drama workshop or ballroom dancing might be especially appropriate.

- is it to gain confidence? Public speaking or self-defence might be suitable.

- is it to be creative, in which case the course might be pottery, sculpture, art and fashion design, or cake decoration?

- are you interested in sharing your own knowledge, as well as learning, in which case the University of the Third Age (see page 96) might be the place to go?

- is there a subject which has always interested you, in which case what is it?

- is it to make a holiday abroad more enjoyable?

As for the question which many people thinking about returning to study ask, about the risk of making a bit of an exhibition of oneself in front of others who may know more, the answer is quite emphatic: don't be anxious. We are all in the same boat and people running adult education programmes are very sensitive to the special needs of older students in the classroom.

Informal, Practical Courses

The main organizers of our first kind of learning, the informal classes or group activies with a learning content, are the local education authorities, which have a responsibility in law to provide them. Classes may also be run directly by voluntary societies, and there is now an increasing number of centres which provide short courses in a residential setting.

Evening institute courses are the ones most likely to be found near to us. The list from the prospectus of one evening institute indicates the diversity of classes which can be taken:

- art and allied subjects for all levels of ability, from complete beginners to those who wish to develop advanced skills.

- basic education in English and mathematics.

- fashion and creative crafts, for example, leather work, dressmaking, pattern cutting.

- food studies, with a range of cookery classes.

- languages, including Dutch, French, German, Greek, Italian, Japanese, Portuguese, Spanish.

- liberal studies in health, the family, local history.

- physical education, sport, and dance from ballroom dancing to aerobics. Some groups have a therapeutic element and are designed for people recovering from illness.

Obviously, the range of classes will depend upon the size of the community for which they are provided. A small evening institute in a rural community will have less scope than one in a crowded inner-city area.

Local authority classes usually take place in evening institutes, schools, community centres, art colleges, technical institutes or other recognized centres of further education which have the facilities and equipment needed for the particular subjects being taught. Most of the classes take place in the evenings, although there are now many classes in the mornings and afternoons, designed for retired people. In London and a number of other cities, classes may take place during the midday lunch breaks. In one or two places there are centres which have been designed exclusively for retired students.

Although attendance records are kept, and there are rules about the minimum number of people who must be registered before a class can be started, the atmosphere at sessions is very informal. There are usually plenty of opportunities for socializing with members of different groups who are using the centre at the same time, which is likely to be offering other activities as well and where there are canteen facilities. All this makes the process of learning very relaxed. The shy and diffident student should find a place in which to be comfortable, and there are plenty of opportunities for exploring different subjects.

The fees for classes in this category, which have a strong recreational emphasis, are usually quite modest. This does not mean the classes are less valuable than those with a more academic bias, but that their primary purpose is with the enrichment of life. That, in itself, is a fundamental function of the educational process, a fact not always understood by children who often tend to see it merely as a means of preparing to earn a living.

'Cultural' Courses

Classes in the second group are generally concerned with what can be described as a cultural or an intellectual exercise. The standards of tuition will be high and students will be expected to maintain their efforts through regular attendance and probably to undertake some homework. Courses may involve a certain amount of written work. For example, the outcome of a year's course on local history might be the joint production of a publication on the locality in which its members live, or perhaps an exhibition of memorabilia.

In this context, oral history is becoming a very popular activity with many older people who may often be the guardians of our heritage. This means that even our limited personal memories are valuable. If it had not been for the people born before the 1914-1918 war, who took part in a national footpath survey organized through their local Parish Councils, many ancient rights of way, which they could remember from their childhood and which had wrongly been ploughed up by farmers, might well have been lost for ever.

So classes which can be very informal, but which combine study with a practical outcome, may provide the stimulus to launch into a new hobby. For example, a class learning about the structure of short-story writing might lead some of the people attending to start writing their own, or a play reading group might sow the seeds for a drama club.

Higher Education Courses

Almost all universities have extra-mural departments, some of which are now called Schools of Continuing Education. They arrange courses during term time, during both afternoon and evening sessions, as well as shorter courses during the vacations. They normally run for up to twenty weeks and meet weekly. Students are expected to undertake a certain amount of written work.

The range of subjects taught varies widely. At London University, for example, there are over 800 part-time courses ranging from astronomy to philosophy. Some courses offered by extra-mural departments lead to diplomas or degrees.

Classes leading to an academic recognition can also be followed through the Open University, where they usually comprise a number of units which can be taken separately. In this way, credits for the final result gradually build up. On average, students may take between six and eight years to complete a full degree course, but there is no need to enter into a long-term commitment, and the range of courses which can be followed is very wide.

Students at the Open University come from a very wide range of backgrounds. The oldest course member the University knows about was 93. Many students are holding down full-time jobs or bringing up a family while they study from a choice of 130 different courses. For example, Harriet, who studied social sciences, was a former clerk and mother of two nearly grown-up children; she wanted to get back to work and find a more satisfying career. David, on the other hand, was a former railwayman who did not intend to vegetate when he retired, so took a course in geology to satisfy a life-long interest in the landscape.

Open University teaching is by a combination of broadcast and television lectures, written work marked by a tutor and, once a year, a residential meeting with a larger group.

Apart from the courses which lead to a degree, the Open University offers a number of short vocational or general interest courses through its continuing education or associate student programme. They are geared to people who want a challenge, but not a degree. They are based on study packs, which combine written material with video cassettes. There are about two hundred to choose from, covering a very wide range of subjects, including retirement planning.

The costs of Open University courses vary widely. A few local authorities will provide financial assistance to students. There is no upper age limit for registering, and no academic qualifications are required.

Another approach to teaching through television is the Open College which functions in a rather similar way to the Open University, but where the emphasis is more on technical skills than academic knowledge. Open College courses are generally more appropriate for young people, though there are some which might well interest more mature students, including one on using a computer. The television programmes are shown on Channel Four, with extensive back-up material provided.

The BBC also provides a wide range of programmes, on

both radio and television, as part of its contribution to continuing education. These programmes are likely to be presented in series and many of them are supported by reading matter which has been specially prepared to help viewers or listeners get the most out of the series.

University of the Third Age

This is an interesting new development in self-help which originated in France. Its educational activities are both organized and attended by people in retirement who may register as students, but who can also bring their own knowledge and skills as teachers. It is learning for its own sake, with no formal qualifications required or offered.

Volunteer members run the University of the Third Age in every way. It is open to anyone who is retired, or unemployed. There are no tests for admission, and no upper age limits. Membership fees vary in different parts of the country, but they are quite modest.

Residential Courses

A number of organizations provide residential courses. Many university extra-mural departments run weekend schools and longer courses in the summer, and there are also residential centres throughout the country organized by local education authorities, and sometimes by voluntary societies.

A full list of what is available is published twice a year by the National Institute for Adult Education (see page 97). It contains information about over 2,000 courses.

Some study tours go abroad to help in learning a language, to explore antiquities, or other appropriate activities. These tours, which combine holiday and study, are also provided by Saga Holidays and its associated company, Renaissance Tours, where distinguished experts in the subjects covered travel as guides and lecturers. When courses are offered in conjunction with a holiday tour, there is no pressure on travellers to be involved in every part of the programme.

Some Useful Sources of Information

BBC Educational Broadcasting Services, Villiers House, The Broadway, London W5 2PA, provides details of forthcoming educational programmes and back-up material.

Evening Institutes: enquire at your local education authority offices or public library.

National Adult School Organisation, Norfolk House, Smallbrook Queensway, Birmingham B5 4LJ, can supply information about local 'Friendship through Study' groups throughout the country, often run in members' houses.

National Extension College, 18 Brooklands Avenue, Cambridge CB2 2HN, provides a range of home studies courses listed in its prospectus, *Guide to Courses*.

National Institute of Adult Continuing Education, 19B De Montfort Street, Leicester LE1 7GE, issues a list of all residential colleges twice a year.

Open University, Walton Hall, Milton Keynes MK7 6AG.

Saga Holidays, Saga Building, Middelburg Square, Folkestone, Kent CT20 1AZ.

University extra-mural departments: make enquiries locally.

University of the Third Age, 13 Stockwell Road, London SW9 9AU, will provide addresses of local groups.

Workers Educational Association, 9 Upper Berkeley Street, London W1H 8BY, will provide addresses of local groups.

Relaxing

However much of our time we plan to use in voluntary or paid work, or in pursuing a course of studies during retirement, there will still be plenty left for hobbies and simply leisure pursuits – the libraries are full of the most wonderful reading matter, and a reader's ticket costs nothing to obtain.

Holidays

It is important to remember that holidays, and a change of scene, are just as important in retirement as they were when we were involved in our working careers.

There is a school of thought which suggests that the first thing to do on retiring is to go on a long holiday as a means of making the break between two different phases of our lives, and to help get over any emotional adjustments.

Most specialized holidays for people in retirement are run in off-season periods, to avoid the worst of the crowds and to get the most competitive prices. Holiday packages designed for older people also tend to include more optional extras and activities, from whist and dancing to guided tours, than may be included in younger peoples' holidays.

People suffering from poor health or a disability may find the Holiday Care Service (see page 102) to be a very useful source of information. It provides a series of leaflets about every possible kind of holiday, ranging from skiing for disabled people to farmhouse accommodation. It can also provide volunteers to travel with someone who cannot manage without support. In some cases, the Holiday Care Service can help in finding sources of funds to assist people who could not otherwise afford to travel. Its service is free.

Bargains

Concessions increasingly available to older people on trains, buses, and planes, make many journeys a good deal less expensive than they would otherwise be. British Rail's Senior Citizen's Railcard, available to anyone over sixty, is a real bargain. It does not have to be used very often to get back the modest investment of £15 it costs for a year.

British Airways offers concessions on domestic flights, and many bus and long-distance coach companies are now doing the same thing, so it is always worth enquiring before making a journey about the bargains which may be on offer.

Concessions for older people are also becoming much more widely available at galleries, museums, theme parks, stately homes, zoos and local leisure centres. Cheap seats at theatres and cinemas, usually during matinees, have been offered for many years.

Hobbies

However enjoyable holidays may be, part of their pleasure is in getting back home and of being reminded of the beauty of the countryside right by our own doorsteps, and of the enormous range of enjoyable things which there are to do in our own country, from visiting historic monuments to making replicas of ancient three-masted schooners.

The potential activities which could fall under the heading of 'hobbies' is much too long to list in a short chapter. Almost any human pursuit, carried out in our spare time, might qualify and for many people retirement at last provides the opportunity to give time to an activity which has been neglected for years.

In some cases, retirement simply provides the opportunity of doing more of what we like – gardening, for example. But the garden may not be a joy to everyone, and for older people beginning to suffer from a disability it may be very important to plan an area which is a pleasure, rather than a burden, to work. Advice on how to set about doing this is available from Horticultural Therapy, a charity established to help people derive the maximum benefit from the garden, even in the most difficult circumstances (see page 102).

There are also several societies which can help to make gardening into a more interesting and, as far as vegetables are concerned, a more profitable pursuit. Unless gardening gives pleasure to only one partner in a marriage, tending it should be shared in just the same way that housework or cooking should be shared.

The approach of retirement also provides an opportunity for couples to plan to launch a new activity together. It does not have to be very expensive or spectacular. For example, visiting bird sanctuaries or nature reserves involves little more than a pair of stout shoes, binoculars, and a book about the different species to be seen.

On the other hand, some hobbies can actually save money, and even earn a modest income. The owner of a knitting machine may provide family members with a regular supply of woollen garments at Christmas, as well as undertaking a few paid commissions for friends, or for specialized boutiques.

Activities which are carried out at home, and which occupy a certain amount of space, may find a welcome base in the additional bedrooms which become available when children are safely out of the nest. It is much easier to be able to pick something up when the mood takes, rather than have all the business of getting it out of storage each time it is wanted, and then of having to pack it away afterwards.

While some hobbies, like stamp collecting or gardening, are obviously very personal, it is likely that many of them will also have an association of like-minded people, with local groups of enthusiasts, who will always be delighted to welcome a new member. If there isn't a group locally, why not start one up?

Many hobbies can be carried out in the open air as well as in the home, for instance, pebble polishing, in which colourful stones can be collected from certain beaches, and then polished into semi-precious and very attractive jewellery. In this way a summer pastime can be linked with an interesting winter occupation. It can also help to pay for itself.

There is a range of hobbies which reflect personal skills and private moments but which also offer the possibility of group activities from time to time. Painting and photography are two examples of interests which can also benefit from relationships with others to compare notes, arrange exhibitions, or to organize technical exchanges.

Music-making and drama represent activities in which social companionship is an essential feature. They also provide opportunities for participants to work behind the scenes: we do not all have to be leading men and women to make the show a success. Scenery and costumes have to be made, lighting fixed, tickets sold, and the show promoted.

Keeping a pet can be a source of great pleasure, and some

passing moments of irritation, at any time of life. It can also be therapeutic, since animals provide companionship and they do not answer back. They also provide an important physical contact for people who are alone. Dogs have an added advantage, since they also require their owners to keep on walking.

However, in planning for a long retirement, it is as well to consider the difficulties owning an animal may present. For example, they are not permitted in some sheltered housing schemes nor in some blocks of flats. There is also the question of what to do with them when you are planning to go abroad. Boarding kennels and catteries are quite expensive establishments.

Of course, there is a great deal of animal and bird life just outside our back door which can provide continuing interest and pleasure, if we make them welcome and feed them when it is appropriate.

The Royal Society for the Protection of Birds (see page 102) has a great deal of interesting information available and it owns considerable areas of land where birds can be watched. It even sells a range of bird feeders, although it should be noted that not all of them are squirrel-proof. But then for some people watching squirrels is itself an entertaining pastime.

For people who enjoy spending time out-of-doors there are a number of opportunities for combining work with pleasure through the local history societies, naturalist trusts, conservation societies and Ramblers' groups which exist in most areas.

For someone who has no burning ambition to pursue a *particular* hobby, but feels he would like to be doing something, a useful introduction might be to visit the various hobbies exhibitions which are held in most towns, to go to open days at art schools, and to visit the library where there will not only be books describing particular hobbies, but possibly a directory of the local societies in the district.

Whilst no-one would want to invest too much money in trying out something which may not develop into a lasting interest, there will almost certainly be enough enthusiasts around who, once contacted, will be glad to demonstrate their own equipment and knowledge to a potential recruit.

Useful Sources of Information

British Rail, Euston House, 24 Eversholt Street, London NW1 1DZ, for information about its 'Senior Citizen's Railcard and other concessionary travel schemes. Leaflets are also usually available at railway stations.

English Heritage, PO Box 71, Bromley, Kent BR1 1LB, manages over 350 historic sites.

Holiday Care Service, 2 Old Bank Chambers, Station Road, Horley, Surrey, RH6 9HW, provides expert advice and information about specialist holiday provisions for disabled and elderly people.

Horticultural Therapy, Goulds Ground, Vallis Way, Frome, Somerset BA11 3DW, helps people who are disabled or elderly to manage their gardens, either through a postal advisory service or by a visit from a personal counsellor.

National Express Ltd, Ensign Court, 4 Vicarage Road, Edgbaston, Birmingham B15 3ES, for information about concessionary travel on express coaches.

National Society of Allotment and Leisure Gardeners, Hunters Road, Corby, Northants NN17 1JE, promotes horticultural education and encourages the establishment of local groups.

Recreation and Leisure Department of your local authority.

Royal Horticultural Society, Vincent Square, London SW1P 2PE, runs the Chelsea Flower Show and several gardens, arranges lectures and demonstrations for members, and publishes a magazine.

Royal Society for Nature Conservation, The Green, Nettleham, Lincoln LN2 2NR.

Royal Society for the Protection of Birds (RSB), The Lodge, Sandy, Bedfordshire SG19 2DL.

Going on Working

For some people the financial stresses of retirement, with its loss of income, come as a serious blow; for others it may be the absence of the stimulus of going to work, or the companionship which goes with it, which leaves a vacuum.

In either case, the solution may lie in a second career, possibly on a part-time basis, or in the launching of a modest personal enterprise of one sort or another. If the latter course is chosen, it is very important to approach the possibility in an objective and businesslike way. For example, the popular but somewhat romantic vision of running a country post-office and store, often regarded as a dream retirement occupation, may turn out to be a good deal less attractive in the harsh reality of unending early morning starts and demands for constant availability during long hours producing diminishing returns as the superstores attract customers away.

It is also important to hold on to the fact that retirement is supposed to be about a transition to a more relaxed and less demanding life, rather than one dominated by the pressures associated with a working life. That is another reason why thoughts about taking on a new job, or of investing in a business, with all that it entails, need to be very carefully weighed up beforehand. It may be a good deal easier to get into it, than it would be to part company with it conveniently.

However, there *are* many possibilities for a continuing paid occupation in retirement, if we want to pursue them. They are certainly well worth exploring, against a background in which recent trends leading to early retirement and redundancy may begin to shift in favour of the older worker, as the impact of a declining birthrate begins to reach the employment market. If, as seems likely, this trend continues in the foreseeable future, increasingly attractive proposals for workers to remain in work or to return on terms to suit our personal circumstances may well increase. Already, numbers of major employers are beginning to acknowledge the inherent reliability of middle-aged staff.

The first step when considering the possibility of going back to work is to ask what is our motivation? If it is chiefly to augment our income, it is very important to establish that a combination of tax demands, and loss of benefits, will not offset most of the financial benefit we expect to gain. It may simply not be worthwhile.

Next, it is important to establish what we actually feel about work itself. If our job was stimulating, we may be glad enough to continue doing it; but if it was boring and tedious, retirement may provide the opportunity to escape from its dull routine. In this case, we may want to look for something quite different. As work is increasingly going to involve more use of high technology equipment, and to have less to do with human relationships, a retirement occupation bringing us into regular contact with a variety of people may come as a refreshing change.

If our regular job involved considerable responsibility, it may be a relief to find something which makes less demands. Management may provide material rewards; but there is often a heavy personal price to pay for being in charge, with deadlines to meet and standards to maintain.

There are other factors about past work which may influence attitudes towards any possible future association with the same employer. For example, was it a generally happy working environment where people, at all levels, respected each other, or was it full of tensions and undercurrents of unrest? Is the company's future reasonably secure, or is it likely to be at the receiving end of a take-over with a consequent shake up of everything and everybody?

All these factors are important, because although it may not be too difficult to launch into a 'retirement career' early on, when we are still in our fifties or sixties, it may well become progressively more difficult to make a second or third career later on. That is why early planning is so important.

One solution to this particular problem of creating a secondary working career in retirement, which a number of people are finding very fulfilling, is to take on a number of smaller assignments. Together, they can represent a flexible package which can be adapted to meet our changing needs as we grow older. Of course, this possibility depends on our ability to offer a service which is marketable through a number of different outlets. In most cases, this will be the case, and an attractive feature of becoming a 'contractor' of one sort or another, lies in the fact that we effectively become our own boss.

Taking on a number of part-time assignments also allows us to work when it suits us, within reason. This, in its turn, makes it possible to organize our leisure time and, in many cases, it may offer the possibility of undertaking some work from home. There is no doubt this is going to become quite general in the future, with computer terminals in our sitting rooms!

So, the first thing to do if we are seriously looking for work is to let as many people as possible know that we are in the market, and what we are prepared to do. Many of our friends and contemporaries may be able to help us, if they themselves are in positions of responsibility.

Apart from word of mouth, the small advertisement boards outside neighbourhood shops are a good source of information about what is already on offer, and where we can describe our own availability. Local newspapers also provide an invaluable source of information, both because of their job advertisement columns, but also because they provide a very effective early warning system about what is likely to happen in the district. For instance, a story about a planning application for a new factory or shopping centre may provide leads.

Job Centres are a useful source of information; they are not only concerned with full-time employment. There are also the offices of the Professional and Executive Register, usually known by its initials, PER. This is another service run by the government which provides openings to work in the professional, executive, scientific and technical services. PER publishes a weekly, Executive Post, which lists job vacancies.

There are some placement agencies for older workers run by voluntary organizations, and here the local Age Concern group may be helpful. It may also have part-time work which it can itself offer. If there is a local Retirement Association, it too should have some ideas about prospects. There are also a few commercial agencies which specialize in finding work for older people.

As it may be some time since we last applied for a job, it is very important to prepare a clear record of our past employment career, skills and qualifications. Two golden rules in this context are not to make any CV too long, and not to leave out long periods in a working life without an explanation. Employers will automatically wonder what is being hidden!

It is also important to provide testimonials. These can include open statements from past employers, as well as the names of referees, to whom prospective employers can go if they wish; but referees should always first be asked if they are prepared to act in this way. Most people are perfectly ready to do so, but get irritated if they are taken by surprise.

It may be as well to prepare a basic letter, which can be varied to suit particular circumstances. It certainly needs to be well presented. The library will have books of advice about job-hunting, and older grandchildren may be very helpful if they have recently been shown how to do things by the careers service at school or college.

Although professional career counsellors are usually associated with the provision of vocational guidance for young people at the thresholds of their major career, they can also be helpful to mature clients considering a new direction in retirement. They will also be able to give advice about the practical elements involved in job hunting.

Starting Up In Business

Any decision about starting our own business really depends upon how much income we are looking for; how much time we are prepared to put into a new enterprise; the amount of capital we have to spare; and the risks we are prepared to take. So before exploring the possibilities in any detail, there are some crucial questions which must be answered:

■ have you had very full discussions with your wife or husband, and with any other members of your immediate family? It is surprising how many demands a small business can make on a large number of people.

■ are you prepared to work a seven-day week?

■ are you being realistic about your health and stamina? Running a small business can be very tiring, and days off for sickness are difficult to organize.

■ if you are thinking of doing a totally new line of business, do you really have the necessary experience? If not, it may be sensible to learn from someone who already knows the ropes.

■ is there an appropriate training course which you might take to prepare you?

■ do you have experience of costing and book-keeping?

■ have you taken on an accountant in whom you have confidence?

■ have you studied how VAT works?

■ have you worked out a proper business plan?

■ do you have sufficient capital to carry you through the initial period, when there will be no profits on which to draw?

■ would a partnership, in which both the risks and profits are shared, make sense?

■ have you got a marketing strategy about whom you are hoping to attract as your customers? Do you know where they are to be found and how they can be contacted?

■ what evidence do you have that the market is really expanding, and there is room for a newcomer?

■ what about the opposition? Have you made a study of who your competitors are likely to be, and how you can make your own product, or services, more economic and attractive than theirs?

■ And, finally, perhaps the most important question of all, are you prepared for the venture to *fail,* in which case you may lose your investment? Of course, failure will be a disappointment, but what will the loss of capital to do your retirement plan as a whole? Some people are natural risk-takers, but it is always better to avoid gambling, if we cannot afford to lose.

If the answers to these questions are generally positive, there are quite a number of potential sources of help. To start with those in the locality: the local council will have information about the size and make-up of the local population; the public library will have plenty of reference books and trade directories; and the Chamber of Commerce should also provide a helpful introduction.

The Small Firms Advisory Service, run by the Department of Trade and Industry, is a very useful source of help, and so is the Council for Small Industries in Rural Areas (COSIRA) (see page 110). Both these organizations will be able to provide experienced people as consultants who will be able to help to assess the market and devise a realistic marketing plan.

The DTI's Small Firms Advisory Service offers an information and counselling service on every aspect of general business administration run through a national network of local centres. It also arranges advice days at Job Centres. The information service is free, and the counselling service is free for the first three sessions. After this, there is a modest charge. The counsellors, who are themselves business men and women, give practical advice on a confidential basis.

There are several possible sources of financial help with a new business, apart from the usual bank loans, hire purchase, or stock financing schemes. The Rural Development Commission, which is now a part of COSIRA, may be able to provide loans to small businesses in rural areas for buildings, plant and equipment.

The government's Enterprise Allowance provides limited financial help, for up to a year, for people who have been out of work for more than eight weeks, and who are under the state retirement age. Some local authorities give practical assistance to small companies, and small firms working in recognized Development Areas may be eligible for Regional Enterprise grants.

All the possibilities should be explored, with the help of professional advice. Loans and grants may be welcome at the beginning, when they appear to solve a problem; but repayments have to be sustained, and often quite tough conditions have to be met.

For people who are looking for a ready-made business, franchises may provide a relatively painless introduction but unless the business in question is part of a well-known and reputable network, it is very important to involve a lawyer to help read the small print. This is a field in which a number of catch-penny schemes have been launched to attract the unwary investor.

Some Useful Addresses
Age Concern groups locally may be able to help in job finding.
Age Endeavour, Willowthorpe, High Street, Stansted Abbotts, Ware, Herts SG12 8AS, helps find part-time work.
Association of British Chambers of Commerce, 212a Shaftesbury Avenue, London WC2H 8EW, for general information, or if you cannot find the address of your local Chamber of Commerce.

British Franchise Association, 75A Bell Street, Henley-on-Thames, Oxfordshire RG9 2BD, will provide information about the range of franchise possibilities.

Council for Small Industries in Rural Areas (COSIRA), 141 Castle Street, Salisbury, Wiltshire SP1 3TP, runs a consultancy service and can provide loans.

Department of Employment, Small Firms and Tourism Division, Steel House, Tothill Street, London SW11H 9NF, provides an information and counselling service.

Department of the Environment, Distribution Section, Building 3, Victoria Road, South Ruislip, Middlesex HAA ONZ, publishes a free booklet, *Planning Permission for Small Businesses: a Step by Step Guide*.

Department of Trade: look in appropriate telephone directory for nearest Regional Office.

Institute of Chartered Accountants in England and Wales, PO Box 433, Chartered Accountants' Hall, Moorgate Place, London EC2P 2BJ, or the **Institute of Accountants,** 27 Queen Street, Edinburgh, EH2 1LA, can help in finding local accountants.

Institute of Marketing, Moor Hall, Cookham, Berks, runs courses and can advise on consultants.

National Federation for the Self-Employed and Small Businesses Ltd, 140 Lower Marsh, London SE1 7AE.

Pre-Retirement Association, 19 Undine Street, London SW17 8PP, publishes a free leaflet about work in retirement. Send a large sae.

Professional and Executive Register: enquire at your local Job Centre.

Regional Development Agencies: look in appropriate telephone directory.

Success after Sixty, 40-41 Bond Street, London W1X 3AF, places older workers in jobs.

FOUR

Keeping Well

There is absolutely no reason why most of us should not enjoy good health as we grow older. Doctors who say to us in later life, 'What else do you expect at your age?' are not doing their job properly. They are there to treat us and to tell us how to prevent further deterioration if things start to go wrong.

On the other hand, it is no good expecting the doctor to wave a magic wand to extend our active life, and there is no elixir which will give us the gift of eternal youth.

Keeping healthy in retirement is largely up to us. There are several ways in which we can assist the process:.

- eat a balanced and varied diet.

- maintain a desirable weight.

- exercise regularly.

- do not smoke.

- drink alcohol in moderation.

- get enough sleep.

- allow time for rest and relaxation.

- stay involved with family and friends.

- keep active through a combination of interests.

- avoid over-exposure to the sun and cold.

- practise good safety habits at home to prevent accidents.

111

Perhaps above all, we need to have a positive attitude towards life. We should *expect* to live a long time. As other chapters have suggested, we should plan ahead for our financial security, as far as we can, as well as for where we are going to live. We should also find out what makes us happy, and then do it. That's probably the best medicine!

This chapter is not intended to be a detailed health-care manual, nor does it catalogue those sad and painful conditions which some people encounter in retirement. In common with diseases which may strike us at any time in our lives, they stem from conditions within our makeup, over which we have no control. It is only by advances in medical science that they may eventually be eliminated, although even when they are severe, modern approaches to care and treatment can often reduce stress.

Accidents

Accidents rarely just 'happen' by chance. Many could have been prevented; but they tend to become more frequent, and more serious, in later life. That is why attention to safety is so important.

There are several reasons why older people may be more prone to accidents. Poor eyesight and hearing can both reduce our awareness of hazards. Then, there are some diseases in later life which lead to unsteadiness. That is why it is important to know what the hazards are and to plan to prevent them whenever possible.

A preoccupation with personal problems can be very distracting. There is no doubt that accidents are sometimes an expression of unhappiness. This makes it doubly important to keep physically and mentally well, and to build in a safety mechanism called 'self-preservation'. It is there by nature in some of us, but not in everyone: some people may need to work at it quite hard.

Another hazard stems from an excess of medication, or a mix of medicine and alcohol. This can make us drowsy and less alert to possible dangers including falls.

Falls are, in fact, the most common cause of serious injury in later life. One of the best ways of avoiding them in the home is by ensuring that you have adequate and suitable lighting. Another precaution is to avoid standing on insecure stools to reach high shelves – the other major cause of accidents in the home.

Food and Drink

There are many publications about good food and how to prepare it available today, most of them with special reference to our changing dietary needs as we grow older. That is why we have concentrated in this section on giving some basic reminders about the beneficial effects which a sensible diet can have on the quality of our lives in retirement. As in any other aspect of this book, it is possible to see how planning – in this case, our diet – can add years to life, as well as life to years.

The same thing applies to drinking. Alcohol can be a genuine social pleasure, but when taken in excess, for whatever reasons, it can destroy not only the lives of those who abuse it, but also the people with whom they live and who love them. But even when the prospects seem bleak, it is never too late to effect an improvement.

Alcohol

Excessive drinking in later life is a more serious problem than many people recognize. It is neglected too often.

Retirement itself may help to hide the problem. In some cases, the idea that it does not matter so much in later life can lead to unnecessary difficulties.

Alcohol slows down the brain and reduces mental alertness. It also affects judgment, physical co-ordination and reaction time. So it increases the risk of falls and accidents.

Over a long period of time, heavy drinking can cause permanent damage to the brain, as well as to the liver, heart, kidneys and stomach; but it can also affect the body in unusual ways by making some problems more difficult to diagnose. For instance, it might mask pains which are an early warning sign of an impending heart attack.

Alcohol, which is itself a drug, mixes very badly with other drugs, whether they are prescribed or just bought over the counter.

People who drink to excess in later life may have always used alcohol heavily, or they may start drinking because of some unhappiness in retirement itself. In this case, alcohol is probably first used to provide temporary relief. Then it becomes a more lasting problem.

Of course, not everyone who drinks heavily has a problem, and the metabolism of a man may give him a slightly higher capacity for alcohol than a woman has, but some of the following symptoms may well be among the danger signs for both men and women:

- drinking to calm nerves or reduce depression.

- loss of interest in food.

- drinking too fast.

- lying about the amount drunk.

- drinking alone.

- getting drunk more than very occasionally.

- frequently getting irritable or unreasonable when not drinking.

- beginning to experience unexpected medical, social, or financial problems which are difficult to account for.

If these symptoms can be identified, and the problem acknowledged, there is no reason why it should not be controlled sensibly.

Diet

Many people in later life are attracted by advertisements for vitamins and minerals which suggest they will improve our appearance, give our sex life a boost, prevent or cure diseases, and even prolong life itself. Unfortunately, there is all too often little scientific evidence to back most of these inflated claims.

Doctors may sometimes prescribe dietary supplements to correct deficiencies in patients, but far too often people take high doses of supplements of various minerals and vitamins without a doctor's advice, in the hope they will prevent or cure a disease. At best, this is probably a waste of money. At worst, particularly if taken to extremes, it can be a real threat to our health.

While scientists have identified a number of nutrients which are essential for our good health, the best way to get what we need is through a well-balanced diet. It has been suggested that we should try to include in our daily diet at least two servings of milk or dairy products such as cheese, cottage cheese or yogurt; two servings of protein-rich foods, such as lean meat, poultry, fish, eggs, beans, or nuts; four servings of fruit and vegetables, including a citrus fruit or juice and dark-green leafy vegetable; and four servings of breads and cereal products (ideally made with whole grain or enriched flours), rice or pasta.

Food

For most of us, eating is one of the pleasures of life; for all of us, it is the critical source of nourishment and energy. We enjoy the taste, the smell, the colour and the texture of foods. Meal times also provide an opportunity of relaxing and enjoying interesting conversation.

Even more important, eating well and regularly each day helps us to keep both active and healthy. Conversely, a poor diet can result in a whole range of problems including lack of energy, malnutrition and bad health.

Although we may well find we want to eat less in quantity as we begin to get older, it is unfortunate that some people in retirement also begin to eat poorer quality food. Sometimes this is because they cannot afford to buy better, but it is also often because they begin to care less about what they eat. This may apply especially to men who live alone and who lose interest in eating when faced with difficulties in buying and preparing food.

It certainly need not be like this when the range of prepared, chilled, and deep-frozen foods available to us is so appetizing and nutritious. Today's detailed labelling of the contents of food, and the instructions on how it should be stored and cooked are particularly helpful, enabling us to balance the prepared foods with the fresh fruit and vegetables we also need.

A balanced and varied diet should involve an intake of calories which equals the amount we burn up in our activities. It is also now generally accepted that we should eat less fat (especially animal fat) and more fibre, and probably cut down on salt and sugar.

There are many excellent publications, both books and magazines, about sensible diet in later life now available. They are well worth reading in retirement.

Our new way of life will have a bearing not just on what we eat, but on when we have our meals as well. Our routine may be very different from the one to which we were accustomed at work.

Eating in retirement will need adjustments by both partners. Some women enjoy spending time in the kitchen; others are just waiting to escape from it, as part of *their* retirement plan. As a result, genuine compromises have to be made about the amount of time to be spent in preparing food, the number of hot meals a day which someone has to produce, and about who is to clear up afterwards! It is very important to establish a workable new routine early on, before the mould is too firmly set.

Digestion

Many of us experience twinges of indigestion as we grow older, but most of the time the system seems to work reasonably well. As time goes on, we begin to discover the foods which are best avoided – especially in the evening.

The surest way to keep the digestive system on an even keel is to:

- eat a well-balanced diet.

- eat slowly, and wherever possible try to relax for 30 minutes after each meal.

- exercise regularly.

- drink alcohol in moderation.

- avoid large amounts of caffeine (remember tea, as well as coffee, contains caffeine).

- be sparing with medicines and pills bought over the counter, and always follow the doctor's instructions when taking prescribed medication.

As with any other condition, do not put off going to see the doctor if something seems to be going wrong.

Keeping In Good Shape

There is no doubt that our lives in retirement will be more enjoyable if we keep in good shape. Exercise, in the form of a sport involving other people, can be a pleasant pastime and can lead to new friendships.

Now is actually a very good time to start up something new, with leisure and well-equipped sports centres opening up in most parts of the country. There have never been so many opportunities, whatever our age. As long as we are sensible in treating our bodies with respect and do not over-do things, we should be able to plan for many active years ahead.

The importance of exercise in keeping our bodies working

as well as possible is now generally accepted. There is no doubt that the human body can both repair and improve itself to an amazing degree. Even people with quite severe disabilities can take part in programmes of moderate exercise to considerable effect, although anyone who is at all unwell should take professional advice about the extent of exercise which can safely be undertaken.

We know about the regular exercises, such as walking, swimming or bicycle riding, from which we can benefit and enjoy at the same time, but there are plenty of other possibilities too, ranging from aerobic dancing to yoga, thanks to the widespread development of sports and leisure centres.

Whatever we do, it must be tailored to our own needs and capacity. Jogging, for example, certainly is not right for everyone; for anyone with unsuspected heart disease it will be positively dangerous.

First of all, it is just as well to consider what benefits can flow from regular sustained exercise. It can strengthen our heart and lungs, our bone and our muscles; lower blood pressure; and act as a protection against the onset of diabetes in later life. Diabetes, which is common in later life, can be an unwelcome result of a sendentary, exerciseless lifestyle in earlier life.

When exercise is combined with a good diet, it can help us lose weight, or maintain our preferred weight, by burning up excess calories. It also gives more energy, helps us sleep, reduces tensions, and may well improve our physical appearance and our general sense of well-being.

But however beneficial exercise may be, it is a mistake to try and do too much straight away, if we have been very sedentary in our habits before retirement. It is also very important to choose an activity which we like. Swimming can be a great pleasure, but continuously going into a pool and completing more and more lengths, with less and less personal contact with anyone else, can get quite boring.

Retirement, of course, provides the perfect opportunity of

taking up a new activity with our partner. The golf course and the tennis court are two ideal settings for a pair to start from scratch.

The Sports Council ran a campaign for some years called 'Fifty plus – all to play for'. It suggested that many of us miss out, simply because we feel we are too old, flabby, or unfit; are frightened of making a fool of ourselves; do not have the money; or simply cannot be bothered. It listed some dos and don'ts before launching into a new sport:

■ do be patient, choose one extra activity at a time and aim for gradual improvement.

■ do exercise a little harder and for a little longer each time – it may take months to reach your goal.

■ do wear comfortable clothes (loose-fitting and non-synthetic).

■ do wear sensible shoes (well-cushioned soles, lace-ups).

■ do warm up, warm down, and avoid very hot showers.

■ do keep a 'progress' diary to encourage yourself.

■ don't take vigorous exercise out of doors in extreme temperatures, or if you have 'flu or a feverish cold.

■ don't try to run before you can walk a mile in 15 minutes.

■ don't let anyone persuade you to do more than feels comfortable.

■ don't select a strenuous sport until you are fit.

■ don't ignore signals to stop if you feel over-tired, sick or unwell. Stop exercising.

Most important – enjoy your exercising.

Physical Well-Being

There are many ways in which we can maintain and improve our health. To begin with, we need to take active steps to prevent discomfort or avoidable suffering. Next, we should maintain our body properly and give its working parts regular checkups, just as we do with our car if we want to keep it on the road in good running order for as long as possible.

Feet

It has been calculated that in the course of a lifetime, our feet will bear a weight equal to several million tons. It is not surprising, therefore, that they begin to ache a bit in later life!

Many of the troubles we encounter with our feet may well result from long years of wear and tear, shoes which are badly designed or which don't fit very well, poor circulation, or toe-nails that are not properly trimmed.

This makes it very important to look after our feet with considerable care as we grow older. Whilst we cannot turn the clock back, it may still be possible to compensate for some of the idiocies of our youthful preference for shoes which looked wonderful, but felt awful.

See a chiropodist at the first sign of trouble, or if clipping your own toe-nails becomes a problem. Chiropody is available through the National Health Service.

Hearing

Poor hearing may well be the most unacknowledged disability from which many people in later life suffer. There is no doubt much more sympathy is often shown to people whose sight is deteriorating than it is to those who are losing their hearing. After all, talking loudly is itself an aggressive form of communication. Part of the trouble stems from the fact that it is so easy to assume people can hear well, because there are few outward signs of hearing loss.

Because of fear, misinformation and, sometimes, mistaken

pride, some people simply refuse to admit that they have a hearing problem, although all the evidence suggests that quite considerable numbers of us will suffer in this way as we grow older. Every year after we are fifty, we lose some of our hearing ability. The decline may be gradual but, like the greying of our hair, it is there all the same.

If hearing problems are ignored, they will certainly grow worse and reduce the quality of our life. It is quite common for people suffering from hearing loss, who have done nothing about it, to begin to withdraw into themselves in order to avoid the frustration and embarrassment of being unable to understand what is being said or to join in conversations.

In some cases, the sense of frustration felt by older people who cannot communicate easily becomes so acute it leads to signs of depression or withdrawal. Such people may even be wrongly diagnosed as 'confused'.

But this is a field in which modern technology has transformed lives, even for those who are profoundly deaf. Help is available through hearing aids which can be very small and unobtrusive, through training, and through medical treatment. At the first sign of a difficulty a doctor should be consulted. There is really no reason to delay.

Some of the early signs of hearing loss are:

- when words are difficult to understand.

- when high notes cannot be heard.

- when there is a continuous hissing or ringing noise in the background or within the ear.

- when another person's speech sounds slurred or mumbled.

- when going out to parties or the theatre, as well as sitting at home watching the television, give less pleasure because of what is being missed.

While people suffering from hearing loss must take the matter into their own hands, there is also much we can do if we have a relationship with a deaf person. We can:

- speak slightly more loudly than usual, but not shout.

- speak at a normal rate, but not too fast.

- speak at a distance of between 3 and 6 feet from the person we are talking to, and position ourselves in a good light so that our lip movements, facial expressions and gestures can be seen.

- if our listener does not understand what we say the first time, then rephrase it.

Perhaps, above all, we should always remember to treat a person with hearing impairment with respect. We should include them in all our discussions about themselves. This will help to prevent a sense of isolation. The title of the BBC programme 'Does he take sugar?' illustrates the way we can all too easily humiliate disabled people.

Sight

Poor eyesight is not inevitable in later life. Whilst some physical changes do take place during the normal ageing process, which can cause a decline in our vision, many older people maintain good eyesight into their eighties and even beyond.

However, as we get older, we probably need a brighter light for reading, cooking, or driving a car. In connection with sight, incandescent bulbs are better than fluorescent lights. Although certain eye disorders and diseases occur more frequently in later life, a great deal can be done to correct these conditions if we take steps in good enough time. So here are three points worth noting:

- we should have regular health check-ups as we grow older to detect such treatable diseases as high blood pressure and diabetes, both of which may cause eye problems.

- we should have a complete eye test every two or three years at least.

- if we experience anything painful, or unusual with our eyes, we should seek advice immediately.

Teeth

Not so long ago most older people would have expected to have lost all their teeth. Now, thanks to fluoride and greater access to dentistry, the majority of us can expect to keep many of our teeth throughout our life. When we are young, the main cause of tooth loss is dental disease. As we grow older, it is more likely to be gum disease.

Care of our teeth is a central element in preventative medicine, which we carry out for ourselves. Even if we have dentures, it is still important to have regular dental check-ups, at least once a year, if not more. If there is any difficulty in finding a dentist ask at the local Family Practitioner Committee, or look at main post offices or public libraries for lists of local dentists. Some dentists will undertake home visits when this becomes necessary.

Sexuality

There is no reason why retirement should not be associated with a continuing active and satisfying sex life, although, especially with men, there may be a gradual slowing of response.

Women generally experience little serious loss of sexual capacity through age alone. The changes which do occur are more likely to result from lower levels of the hormone œstrogen during, and after, the menopause.

However, if problems occur they should not be assumed to be an inevitable part of ageing. They will almost certainly result from disease, reactions to drugs, or possibly to some emotional upset or psychological difficulty and they should be discussed with the doctor or a trained counsellor.

Screening

It is now becoming quite common for people at work to take regular health checks. The purpose of such checks is twofold: to find at an early stage any hidden diseases which do not produce normal symptoms by which they can be recognized, and to provide an opportunity to expose difficulties which might otherwise have remained unacknowledged and untreated. The latter purpose can be particularly relevant when it is retired people having the check-up.

Specific tests which can be carried out during a routine health check include taking blood pressure, in the case of both men and women, and doing cervical smear tests and mammography tests for early detection of breast cancer in women. In addition, the check-up provides the opportunity for our general health to be observed, and for preventative steps to be taken at an early stage, if necessary.

Doctors working in the NHS are required to take an increasing regular interest in their patients who are over 75, and to make contact at least once a year, perhaps through a visit by the practice nurse; but in the early stages of retirement, it is really up to us to prevent things from getting out of hand for ourselves.

Smoking

Cigarette smoking is a major cause of cancer, heart disease, narrowing of the arteries, chronic bronchitis and emphysema, It also contributes to a number of other diseases. It therefore makes sense for us to give up smoking, if we want to plan a long and healthy retirement for our own sake, as well as for the people with whom we live. The partner of a heavy smoker will also be the passive recipient of the damaging fumes.

It is never too late to give up smoking, even after many years. It certainly can be achieved at any age, although obviously the earlier the better. Studies in the United States of America have shown that older people who take up programmes to stop smoking have a higher success rate than those who are younger.

There are many ways of stopping smoking, but no single method works for everyone. Most of us manage to stop as soon as we are really persuaded about the self-inflicted damage we are doing, but some people need the support and encouragement of a doctor, a clinic, or an organized self-help group. Some will suffer from withdrawal symptoms which include taking it out on everyone around; but they pass, and many smokers manage to give up without any withdrawal symptoms at all.

Some ways of helping in the process of giving up smoking are to:

■ launch our change in habit to coincide with retirement, as a part of a new way of life.

■ make it clear to callers that we now live in a no-smoking house.

■ get friends to sponsor us for a set time in aid of a good cause. It will help our motivation!

■ use the money saved to put towards something enjoyable – a holiday perhaps.

■ keep away from smokers as far as possible, especially during the early stages.

■ ask for no-smoking tables in restaurants and for no-smoking bedrooms in hotels.

■ if there are real difficulties, ask the doctor about the use of nicotine chewing gum.

■ if we still find we really need support, consider the possibilities of joining a like-minded group.

Remember too, that cutting down is of little use. The number of cigarettes we smoke will almost certainly creep up every day, and changing to a pipe or cigars will not do the trick either. There is only one solution. If at first we don't succeed, then we must try again!

Some Useful Sources of Advice and Information

Accidents
Royal Society for the Prevention of Accidents (ROSPA), Cannon House, The Priory Queensway, Birmingham B4 6BS, issues printed advice material.

Alcohol
Alcoholics Anonymous, PO Box 1, Stonebow House, Stonebow, York YO1 2NJ, provides a fellowship and local self-help groups for men and women to share their difficulties and work together to solve their common problem.

Alcohol Concern, 305 Grays Inn Road, London WC1X 8QF, provides an information service.

Deafness
British Association for the Hard of Hearing, 7-11 Armstrong Road, London WC2 7JL, provides an advisory and information service, encourages social activities through clubs throughout the country.

The Royal National Institute for the Deaf (RNID), 105 Gower Street, London WC1E 6AH, can give advice on devices to help deaf and hard-of-hearing people

Diet and Food
The British Nutrition Foundation, 15 Belgrave Square, London SW1X 8PS, publishes a free booklet, *Healthy Eating for the Elderly.*

Disability
Disabled Living Foundation, 380-384 Harrow Road, London W9 2HU, has information and displays about a wide range of aids for disabled people, including an incontinence advisory service.
Royal Association for Disability and Rehabilitation (RADAR), 25 Mortimer Street, London W1N 8AB, has a range of material about mobility.

Exercise and Sport
The Sports Council, 16 Upper Woburn Place, London WC1H OQP.

General Health Education
Health Education Authority, 78 New Oxford Street, London WC1A 1AH, issues written material about questions of health.

Sexuality
Age Concern England, Bernard Sunley House, 60 Pitcairn Road, Mitcham, Surrey CR4 3LL, has published *Living, Loving and Ageing – sexual and personal relationships in later life* (£4.95).

Sight
The Royal National Institute for the Blind (RNIB), 224 Great Portland Street, London W1N 6AA, provides an information and advisory service.

Smoking
Action on Smoking and Health (ASH), 5-11 Mortimer Street, London W1N 7RH, can provide information about local groups.

General addresses

Age Concern England, 60 Pitcairn Road, Mitcham, Surrey, CR4 3LL. Telephone (01) 640 5431.

Age Concern Scotland, 33 Castle Street, Edinburgh EH2 3DN. Telephone (031) 225 5000.

Age Concern Wales, 1 Park Grove, Cardiff, South Glamorgan CF1 3BJ. Telephone (0222) 371821/371566.

Age Concern Northern Ireland, 6 Lower Crescent, Belfast BT7 1NR. Telephone (0232) 245729.

Age Concern serves older people through independent local groups providing a range of community services such as lunch clubs, day centres, visiting schemes, transport schemes, family support and other schemes. The national centres campaign to develop and promote improved policies and support and advise the local groups. Look in your telephone directory to find your nearest group.

Help the Aged, 16-18 St James' Walk, London EC1R OBE. Telephone (01) 253 0253.

A major fundraiser. Help the Aged assigns money to support activities both in Britain and overseas. In Britain, the emphasis is on day centres and day hospitals, minibuses, alarm systems, research and education. The information service produces a range of advice leaflets.

The Centre for Policy on Ageing, 25-31 Ironmonger Row, London EC1V 3QP. Telephone (01) 253 1787.

An independent unit which aims to promote better services and policies for older people, providing policy-makers and professionals with research studies, reports and information.